I0824968

Your Turn to Host

A Guide to Great Parties and Gatherings

Your Turn to Host

AMBER MAYFIELD HEWETT

ARTISAN | NEW YORK

Library of Congress Cataloging-in-Publication Data is on file.

ISBN 978-1-64829-445-7 (hardcover)
ISBN 978-1-64829-447-1 (ebook)

Book design by Shubhani Sarkar
Cover design by Nina Simoneaux

Published by Artisan,
an imprint of Workman Publishing,
a division of Hachette Book Group, Inc.
1290 Avenue of the Americas
New York, NY 10104
artisanbooks.com

Printed in China (APS) on responsibly sourced paper

First printing, April 2026

10 9 8 7 6 5 4 3 2 1

To my family, my friends, and my husband, Jordan,
who give me so much to celebrate every day.

And to all the people who host dinner parties,
cookouts, game nights, and get-togethers:
You are the glue of our communities.

CONTENTS

FOREWORD BY THÉRÈSE NELSON 9

INTRODUCTION 11

HOW TO USE THIS BOOK 16

1 Making Your Home a Destination for Gathering 18

2 The Anatomy of a Good Shindig 38

3 Parties at My Place 86

4 The Finer Details 204

AFTERWORD 223

FURTHER READING 226

ACKNOWLEDGMENTS 227

INDEX 228

FOREWORD

The first time I met Amber, she was center stage on a panel of event planners. I was then celebrating my twentieth year as a chef and caterer, so I, like a lot of folks in the room, was accustomed to the tried-and-true tactics that had built all our careers. I guess that's why when Amber, with all her brilliant poise, started speaking her simple truth, the room was primed for her message.

Because she came to event planning with fresh eyes and struck out on her own so early, she had no misguided fidelity to old rules. Amber's vision for her company, To Be Hosted, included, as a central business practice, her sitting fully in her position as a young woman of color. As such, she would bring life, culture, and color to event planning by starting from a creative ether filled with the kith and kin she had watched get overlooked in favor of the more familiar alternatives. Because this network of hers was inherently full of dope, creative, and hungry small-business owners, there was not just equity in this model but profit—and ultimately, superlative events.

This recalibration of the ethical center was the missing piece in the decades-long conversation in hospitality about parity and access. This young woman, not even thirty years old at the time, was able to deploy a wealth of skill to pull off everything from large-scale conference productions to intimate dinner parties. And because her network was so robust, Amber would eventually grow her brand to include a magazine called *While Entertaining* to celebrate and share the bounty of talent she was witnessing. She created five volumes of a joyful, beautifully composed magazine full of celebratory pages heralding the brilliance of the chefs, wine and drink folks, florists, and all manner of artists in her To Be Hosted community. The magazine evolved into a newsletter of the same name, where she continues to share how the pros make their magic. On social media, Amber also offers a series called Soirée School, her master class of tips and event-planning tricks. All this work is the DNA of the book you are about to read.

My first reaction when Amber told me about this book was: *I want the* first *copy.* The book couldn't help being brilliant because it was born out of her profound belief that you should have access to and be inspired by a wider, more colorful range of influences as you plan life's celebrations, from everyday suppers to elaborate events.

Amber Mayfield Hewett is a woman I am proud to call my friend and peer. In this book, she has codified and organized an intensive and insightful plan of action that will make entertaining more joyful for you and your guests. And she has done it with that signature Amber style and grace that we haven't seen since B. Smith gifted us with *B. Smith's Entertaining and Cooking for Friends*. This is a book you will want to give as a gift, to pass down to your children, and to reference often as a companion to your greatest entertaining moments.

—THÉRÈSE NELSON

Chef, writer, and founder of BlackCulinaryHistory.com

INTRODUCTION

WELCOME. I'VE BEEN EXPECTING YOU.

My story starts at the dinner table (as all good stories do). In 2017, I started a supper club called To Be Hosted. At the time, I was in my early twenties, living in Harlem, New York, and working as an assistant at Bravo TV. Like many twentysomethings who move to the big city, I loved going to parties, traversing the city's bustling restaurant scene, and meeting new people. The more I explored, the more I was drawn to restaurants, late-night speakeasies, and members-only clubhouses. I ended up at some incredibly beautiful and buzzy places, but something was always missing. Even though I was surrounded by people all the time, I was lonely. And so I started thinking a lot about feelings of belonging and how those feelings show up in how we gather.

At the same time, my interests were expanding beyond a career in television. I knew it would only be a matter of time before my parents started to question how long I would be capturing social media content for reality TV stars. When I thought about the things I loved (food and parties), the things I needed (passion-driven work and safe spaces), and the things I wanted out of this life (community and enjoyment), all signs pointed toward creating my own supper club. In particular, a supper club that would highlight Black chefs and create experiences where all diners would feel cared for and connected.

When I started To Be Hosted, I planned dinner parties at any location that would welcome us. There was a filmmaker who rented me the basement of his brownstone, and art galleries, coffee shops, and coworking offices that let me use their spaces after hours. For each dinner, I would bring in a chef, an artist, and a musician to be part of the event. I would spend hours thinking about how to weave together each of our perspectives, and I would pore over every detail, from the menu to the table design to the seating arrangements. I wanted to make guests feel like their presence was highly anticipated and important to me—because it was.

I organized my first To Be Hosted dinner party at a coworking space in SoHo. I invited friends, friends of friends, roommates, coworkers, and a few people I had met while out and about in the city. There were twenty-four guests who entered as strangers, but as the night went on, they were laughing and exchanging stories like old friends. We enjoyed a family-style dinner while a cellist played instrumental versions of popular songs (including "Mask Off" by Future). By the end of the night, my perspective on parties, and particularly dinner parties, had completely changed. The experience gave me a feeling I had never felt before. It felt like belonging. It felt like leisure. It felt like pure enjoyment. From that evening onward, my work planning events has been grounded in the belief that great parties bring out the best in people.

Since starting To Be Hosted, I have curated countless dinner parties. Along the way, I became quite good at organizing events. Before long, my expertise was sought after by everyone from rising entrepreneurs, artists, and musicians to top companies and household brands. I have planned cocktail parties, dinner parties, black-tie galas, and even a few weddings. The planning of parties has taken me from brownstones in Harlem to vineyards in Sonoma County, California, from the small village of Cadenet in southeastern France to art galleries in the Shoreditch area of London. The more parties I planned, the more certain I became that I had a special gift that I was meant to share.

I can trace my love of parties and hosting back to my childhood. My mother and her mother were my first examples of great hosts. When I think of my grandmother's house in Teaneck, New Jersey, I think of Easter mornings, after-church luncheons, reunions with cousins, and an overstocked pantry that kept all the grandchildren well fed. And when I think of my parents' house in Nanuet, New York, I think of Christmas dinners, backyard cookouts, team gatherings, and family birthday dinners that would always end with a personalized cake from the local bakery.

When I was growing up, my parents were both teachers; my dad was also a coach (he still is), and my brother and I played sports from as young an age as I can remember. Our family schedule was filled with early mornings, tight schedules, and a lot of shuttling from one activity to the next. But for birthdays and holidays, we always slowed down and made time to gather. We were all home at the same time, and we enjoyed big, bountiful meals together. I grew to love holidays, dinner parties, cookouts, and celebrations for this reason. And I was particularly interested in the careful planning that defined the days and weeks leading up to these events.

Watching my mother and grandmother prepare for our family gatherings fascinated me. Even at a young age, I recognized that their pre-party routines were as much of a ritual as the celebration itself. After observing so intently, I was excited when I was called on to peel sweet potatoes or snap the ends off string beans. I especially loved taking out the "good plates" to set the table while pretending not to listen as my aunts and uncles whispered among themselves. Helping prepare for the family gatherings was actually a really easy way to "get in some grown folks' business," but kitchen gossip aside, I learned that seeing a culture through the lens of its pre-party rituals is a very special thing. There are stories exchanged, techniques and recipes that can only be learned by doing.

When I got older and started hosting my friends and family, I found myself returning to the same pre-party routines that I'd observed my mother and grandmother perform. And I refined these

5
Happy Birthday Amber
Amber

practices when I started To Be Hosted and made party planning my profession.

To take a keen interest in the details of how we host is to have a stake in how we define cultures, how we heal our generations, and how we reaffirm our community bonds. How we eat, what music we listen to, what we talk about, how we make each other feel—these are the ingredients that fuel social camaraderie. This is the true power of hosting and the dynamic responsibility of hosts. And this is what has compelled me to put my experiences down on paper and share my practices with you.

I set out to find a solution for mundane social scenes and lonely Tuesday-night dinners. By dining with strangers, I found my people (a few of them are pictured opposite). I learned about the world, and I learned about myself. When times are good (and when they are bad), I believe we can turn to hosting to keep our loved ones close and make our communities stronger.

In this book, you will find my arsenal of ideas and techniques to help you get the most out of hosting. With care and intention, I've compiled these resources to help you cultivate your own hosting rituals that are fueled by creativity and a sensitivity toward how you make people feel. It's *your* turn to host, and I am honored to be here helping you plan for moments of joy.

Let's get this party started!

HOW TO USE THIS BOOK

Your Turn to Host is for the aspiring host who needs an empowered start as much as it is for the seasoned host in search of some fresh perspective. I want you to turn to this book not as a rigid, one-size-fits-all instruction manual, but as a source for information and inspiration.

We'll begin with Making Your Home a Destination for Gathering (page 18), where we will focus on preparation that supports hosting casually, "effortlessly," and spontaneously.

In The Anatomy of a Good Shindig (page 38), I'll share my comprehensive, step-by-step guide for every piece of the party-planning puzzle. Here is where you will learn to love details, lists, and timelines. And after the preparation, I'll give you my pointers for leading a party artfully, too.

Next, you will find an all-access peek inside Parties at My Place (page 86), where I illustrate how my planning philosophies translate to the parties and get-togethers I host at home. I'll bring you along to events big and small, and offer up a ton of party-specific tips and lessons.

And in The Finer Details (page 204), you will find a collection of resources and recommendations to finalize your party plans.

The Entertaining Journal

I started journaling about my party planning and party experiences very early in my hosting journey. I find that handwriting my plans, musings, and after-party notes is important for setting intentions and maintaining a hosting approach that is carefully considered. In my journal, I preserve recipes, document planning techniques, and archive special stories from events. When I am feeling creatively stuck or uninspired, I return to these entries to reconnect with my tried-and-true practices. Throughout this book, I will reference opportunities to take out your entertaining journal to follow different planning prompts and do reflection exercises. Don't skip this step! Writing down your plans and ideas by hand will lead to more critical and creative thinking.

one

Making Your Home a Destination for Gathering

Hosting is about so much more than parties commemorating momentous occasions. Being a masterful host starts with taking the small, everyday opportunities we have to open our home to others. And so, the start of your hosting journey is preparing a mental and physical space that is encouraging of your entertaining endeavors. When you tell your friends to "just come over" after work, when your in-laws want to drop by, or when a neighbor turns up on your doorstep in need of a listening ear, I want you to be confident when you open your door. In this section, we will prepare your mindset, pantry, and entertaining space for inviting people to come on in (and stay awhile).

The Mindset of a Host	20
A Party Planner's Pantry	22
Curating for the Senses	31
Regular Hosting Rituals	32
For Late Nights & Early Mornings	33

THE MINDSET OF A HOST

There is a degree of intimacy and vulnerability that comes with inviting people into your home and resolving to care for them. In this respect alone, hosting can quickly become quite daunting. For help, you might turn to the internet or social media, where there is no shortage of how-tos, recipes, and inspiration. But as you scroll, in creeps the desire to plan the perfect party and be a formidable host. Soon you are lost at sea, trying to meet some fantastical and unsustainable expectations of a "host with the most." And as you do so, you drift further and further from the one thing that makes hosting special: *you*.

So before we dive in to all the frills and thrills of entertaining, I want to make sure your hosting disposition is anchored to who *you* are and how *you* live, that you are comfortable in your own skin and in your own home. You can't be overly concerned with the "right way" or what is "proper" or "perfect." In fact, if you want to have any confidence and any joy in hosting, you have to take everything you consume about the topic (including this book) with a grain of salt (kosher salt or sea salt, whichever you prefer). Host when it *feels* good. Serve the dishes *you* are comfortable making. Follow the design idea that naturally excites *you*. And let your personal story and style be your North Star, always.

When a host maintains their unique perspective, embraces their own strengths (and weaknesses), and leans fearlessly into hosting their own way, the gathering tends to have a good aura. Behind every great get-together is a host who is making hosting work for them, and not the other way around. You are going to read a lot of tips in the pages to come, but this is the most important one: If you want your gathering to be special for you and memorable for your guests, make it deeply personal.

Discover Your Personal Hosting Style

Grab your entertaining journal and jot down answers to the below questions, designed to help you identify your hosting preferences and tastes.

- What types of experiences and environments make you feel the most energized and confident?
- Do you like being in gatherings that are big and buzzy? Or do you prefer small groups?
- When you imagine yourself hosting, what do you imagine?
- What occasions do you want to host?
- How often do you want to be hosting?
- What design styles and details appeal to you?
- What flavors and menus do you gravitate toward?
- What type of music do you enjoy?

As you write, you should start to have a clearer understanding of your own personal hosting style. Now all you have to do is stay true to it. This does not mean your style won't evolve over time—it can and perhaps should—but return to these questions to make sure this evolution flows with *you* and not with mainstream trends.

A PARTY PLANNER'S PANTRY

The walk-in pantry at my maternal grandmother's house in Teaneck, New Jersey, was filled to the brim with ingredients (spices, Carnation evaporated milk, Jiffy corn muffin mix, elbow pasta, bread, cooking oils), snacks, pots, pans, and utensils. She even made space for a hot comb, an ironing board, a tool kit, and shoe polish. To a child, it seemed large, but as I grew older I recognized that it was pretty humble in size, no more than 5 feet (about 1.5 m) wide and about 4 feet (1.2 m) deep, with shelves that stretched from the doorframe to the back wall. It wasn't picturesque, but that wasn't the point. There was a utility to my grandmother's pantry: Everything had its place, and everything was necessary. When you walked in, it felt like you would find exactly the thing you needed, so long as you knew where to look. Grandma Ruth was always prepared. I like to think this is where I get my natural enthusiasm for things that have a place and a plan.

A pantry represents the spirit of preparation. It is a well-stocked pantry that makes entertaining look "effortless" when in fact there was a significant amount of effort put in—it just took place long before you were under the watchful eyes of your guests. My pantry has become the repository for all the little things that have influenced my approach to hosting: the items that carry my fondest memories, the ingredients and cookbooks used to make the dishes I love to share, and the cook- and serving ware that knows all my secrets.

In this section, I share the timeless tools, well-loved items, and party supplies that have brought ease to my party planning. You should adapt this list to fit your hosting style, the size of your space, how you want to entertain, and whom you want to entertain. For example, if you have a small apartment and a close-knit group of friends, you might focus on collecting an assortment of interesting plates, glassware, and cutlery to use in hosting intimate dinner parties. If you have a large outdoor entertaining space, you might place a greater emphasis on acquiring shatterproof plates, biodegradable cups and utensils, and coolers. If you want to host big family gatherings, your pantry may need to hold snacks and games for children, teens, and adults alike.

Note: This section focuses on items specific to parties and gatherings. You can find an expanded list of kitchen tools and shelf-stable ingredients to complete your pantry on pages 206–207.

THANK YOU

Kitchen Tools

These multipurpose tools will be well utilized when you're preparing for a party. You can find great options at Crate & Barrel and Williams Sonoma.

Aluminum baking sheets. For baking and roasting meats and vegetables. When flipped upside down, a rimmed baking sheet can also be a substitute for a rimless cookie sheet.

Cast-iron skillet (12 inches/30 cm). For pan-searing, sautéing, baking, frying, and so much more. Watching my grandmother, I learned that all good things come from a cast-iron pan. With it, I can make pancakes in the morning and steaks in the evening! When properly cared for, a cast-iron skillet will be with you for decades. Use gentle utensils to avoid scratching; wash while warm, using minimal soap; dry the pan immediately; and condition the pan with cooking oils.

Ceramic casserole dish (9 by 13 inches/ 23 by 33 cm). For pasta bakes, lasagna, focaccia, cakes, bread puddings, and cobblers. Choose a dish with handles that can travel with you or be utilized as an impromptu serving tray when needed. My favorites are from Great Jones and Staub.

Medium Dutch oven. A heavy pot with a lid comes in handy for baking, braising, searing, and frying. It can also be used to serve hot chocolate or cider, or popcorn on movie night.

Ice cream scoops. I recommend a three-pack of stainless-steel scoops in differing sizes with levers for easy release. The range of sizes will allow you to go beyond scooping ice cream, gelato, and sorbet: You'll also be able to evenly portion cookie dough, crab cake mixture, and ground meat for hamburger patties; to form meatballs and falafel; to scoop out the center of seeded fruits and vegetables; and even to proportionately add frosting to cupcakes.

Kitchen blowtorch. You may be tempted to skip this one, but a small culinary torch can be used to toast meringue or marshmallows, caramelize sugar, quickly melt cheese, roast peppers, toast breadcrumbs, and so much more. Torching a dish just before it hits the table is a fun party trick when done confidently.

Ramekins. Ceramic ramekins have a lot of uses around a party. During meal preparation, they can be used to collect ingredients and arrange what chefs call a "mise en place" before you start cooking. They can also be used for baking individual portions of various sweet and savory dishes. On serving platters and welcome tables, ramekins can hold dips, spreads, or sauces. When flipped upside down, they can be used to prop up plates, adding height and dimension to your tablescape.

Salad spinner. For drying greens and herbs, and any other vegetables that you want to dry before cooking or serving.

For the Table

I recommend having at least four place settings more than the number of people you can seat at your dining table(s), so you're covered if anything breaks and always prepared if you have to squeeze in one more guest.

Bowls. Can be used for individual servings or for side dishes during a family-style meal.

Chargers or place mats. Both chargers and place mats contribute to the décor of the table while protecting the table or tablecloth from getting dirty. Which you choose to use depends on your personal taste. Chargers, which are typically made of glass, ceramic, metal, or wood, add a sense of formality to the table and help dishes placed on top retain their heat. Place mats can be used for more casual dinner table settings and come in a variety of materials, including cotton, linen, rattan, and vinyl.

Flatware. Invest in a quality set in your preferred style. Your collection should start with dinner forks, knives, and spoons. Then, depending on your hosting needs (and how much formality you like at your dinner table), you might include salad forks, dessert forks, bread knives, steak knives, soupspoons, and dessert spoons. My set from Lenox has seen me through many, many dinner parties.

Glassware. You can cover your basic needs with these glasses that I affectionately refer to as "my starting five" (as shown below): (1) an old-fashioned glass; (2) a tall tumbler for water, soda, or cocktails; (3) a coupe glass that can be used for cocktails or serving dessert; (4) an all-purpose wineglass; and (5) a Champagne flute.

Linen napkins, tablecloths, and table runners. Start with a neutral color and collect more hues, textures, and designs over time. My favorite sources for these are Anthropologie, Cultiver, and Etsy. You might also want to pick up some napkin holders, rings, or ribbons.

Plates. I recommend having different sizes in your collection—including bread or appetizer plates, salad or dessert plates, and of course dinner plates. I prefer stoneware or hand-crafted ceramic. My tried-and-true set is from Jono Pandolfi (a favorite among restaurateurs as well). You can also find beautiful collections at East Fork Pottery.

For Serving

These items will help you get food and drink to the table for guests. As with the items in all these sections, the style and quantities for these will vary based on how you want to host. I've found my most well-loved items at Anthropologie, Crate & Barrel, West Elm, and Williams Sonoma.

Beverage dispensers and/or pitchers. To serve water and other beverages.

Cake stand. To store and display cakes, pies, and pastries. I like stands with a dome to keep the desserts fresh.

Chafing dish sets. These typically include wire racks, fuel, and full- and half-size aluminum pans. These sets are ideal for serving hot food at large gatherings and cookouts.

Champagne bucket. To chill Champagne or other beverages before serving.

Mesh food covers. To keep insects away when serving food outside. A necessary addition if hosting alfresco is your vibe.

Punch bowl. A great punch bowl has been the centerpiece of some of my favorite gatherings, from church receptions to cookouts to college parties. Choose one large enough that you can fill it with pre-batched beverages, put bottled or canned beverages on ice, or serve large salads, snacks, and desserts.

Serving trays. I love a sturdy tray with handles so I can fill it with appetizers, drinks, or desserts and move through a party to serve my guests. I have a collection of vintage silver trays and glossy lacquered ones. I recommend having two or three, in different sizes and materials.

Serving vessels and utensils. Build a collection of serving plates, platters, and bowls that fit the types of parties you most like to host. You will also need serving forks and spoons, tongs, and pastry servers. For grazing boards, make sure you have appetizer-size serving utensils like cheese knives, teaspoons, honey drizzlers, and canapé forks as well.

Wine decanter. To aerate wine (or let the wine "breathe"), which can enhance its flavor and aroma.

Décor

Maintain a collection of centerpieces and adornments for your table or entertaining space based on what you use most. I believe fresh flowers and candles will always be in style, so the décor section of my pantry is focused on candles, vases, and related accessories.

Candles and accessories. Collect various types of candles (e.g., votives, tapers, and pillars) and have fun with sizes, colors, and textures (e.g., ribbed or fluted, twisted or spiraled, bubbled or honeycombed). I recommend scentless candles for the entertaining space and scented ones for bathrooms and guest bedrooms. When it comes to candleholders, it's again worth collecting a variety of styles, so you have a choice when you are setting up your décor. Candlestick adhesive is helpful to ensure that taper candles are held securely in their holders, and wand-style lighters are ideal for candles in taller holders that can be harder to reach with a match. My favorite candles come from Ester & Erik, Creative Candles, and Etsy.

Vases and floral accessories. Start your collection with at least one large statement vase, three or four midsize vases (depending on the size of your dinner table), and five or six bud vases to hold single blooms in bedrooms and bathrooms or on side tables. If you are limited on storage space or prefer a more casual look, you can also use mason jars, beverage glasses, or cereal bowls as floral vessels. For tools, I recommend floral sheers to cut stems and branches when putting together your floral arrangements and chicken wire or tape to add a support grid to the top of your vases. You can find vases and supplies at Afloral, Jamali Garden, or your local craft store.

Partyware

You can find single-use items (e.g., tableware or décor), including those with holiday, seasonal, or party themes, on Etsy or at your local party supply store.

Biodegradable disposables. This includes plates, cups, utensils, paper or agave straws, and cocktail napkins and larger napkins, for large parties or outdoor entertaining. I also have toothpicks to serve appetizers, create mini skewers, and garnish drinks.

Celebration accessories. This is not a necessity, but I have a reserve of festive candles, confetti, streamers, and party garlands so I am always ready to celebrate my loved ones. I also keep a collection of greeting cards for birthdays, holidays, special occasions, and well-wishes. This is my mom's secret for never forgetting a birthday and being ready when someone shares exciting news or an accomplishment. I also have thank-you notes for the guest who brought an extra-special host gift or stayed late to help clean up.

Special Touches

Beyond supplies for cooking and serving, I also keep a few items on hand for inspiration, entertainment, and guest convenience.

Beloved cookbooks and craft books. To serve as reference for recipes, ideas, and inspiration. Find my favorites in the Further Reading section on page 226.

Entertaining journal. A notebook in which to write down recipes, ideas, to-do lists, shopping lists, and after-party notes.

Games. I love having games for gatherings. My mom always had games stacked up to keep us occupied as kids, teens, and adults. Collect your favorites and add to your collection to accommodate all ages as your entertaining needs evolve.

Mints. Keep them in a jar that guests can reach for after dinner.

To-go containers. For sending leftovers home with guests.

Polaroid
Polaroid
REBEKAH PEPPLER
APÉRITIF
COCKTAIL HOUR
the FRENCH WAY
POTTER
MELCHER MEDIA
THE MARTHA MANUAL
MARTHA STEWART
HMH
THE ART OF GATHERING
Priya Parker
Toni Tipton-Martin
Jubilee
HILL HOUSE LIVING
Paula Sutton
B. SMITH: RITUALS & CELEBRATIONS
BARBARA SMITH
RANDOM HOUSE
RAINBOW

CHAMPAGNE
JEAN DUCLERT
Grand Marnier
BORDEAUX
1947
Old Cider
PRODUIT DE PARIS

CURATING FOR THE SENSES

To design and maintain a home that is fit for a gathering, you have to focus on vibe setting. When you purposefully engage the five senses, you can make choices that lead to a more inspiring atmosphere for gathering. The best way to evaluate the sensory experience of your home is to walk through the front door and take note of the things that capture your attention. Then think about how you can use this "front door impression" to make a guest feel more welcome as they move through your space.

Sight: Beyond having a space that is well put together, make décor choices that will spark curiosity or cue up a fun story that will give your guests an opportunity to get to know you better. You can accomplish this through art (collected or DIY) and objects like textiles, tapestries, sculptures, books, photographs, or unique furniture pieces.

Smell: If the smell of a home-cooked meal is not taking over, make sure you have a signature home fragrance. Choose something personal. At my home, the scent is the fragrance from the hotel that my husband and I stayed at during our honeymoon in Florence, Italy.

Sound: Create and maintain a "house playlist" with all your favorite songs to serve as lively background music. You can turn this playlist on as you cook, clean, and get ready for the party, or when you are hosting a more impromptu or casual gathering. The songs on this playlist should put you in the mood to dance or sing along.

Touch: While guests might not walk around and touch all your surfaces, they will consciously or unconsciously notice the materials that surround them. I've always appreciated that my aunt Dawn keeps a large faux-fur blanket on her living room couch. It immediately communicates that this is a place to get comfortable. Think about what the textures and materials around your home might be conveying to your guests.

Taste: A guest's first sip or bite must be a good one. Stock up on the beverages that you love to share (or the favorites of your frequent guests). You should also consider what foods you want to have on hand for spontaneous gatherings. This might be a go-to appetizer, ingredients for a pasta specialty, or some frozen favorites. At my home, you can always count on a snack plate with cheddar cheese, Port Salut cheese, fig jam, sliced apples, prosciutto, plantain chips, and honey wheat pretzel sticks. And I've likely got some cookie dough tucked in the freezer for us, too.

REGULAR HOSTING RITUALS

In the next section, I'll share all my secrets for hosting when you want to put a little extra razzle-dazzle on the table. Before we dive in to that, I want to spend a little more time on the everyday hosting experiences. So many times, I've found myself saying, "Just come over." And these little gatherings have proven to be exactly what my guests and I needed for connecting, reviving, and even a bit of healing.

Now that you've curated a space you love to be in (and want to share with others), I have a few ideas for those moments when you would like to host (without doing the most). Tell your friends to "just come over" for:

Couchside Café. Invite a few friends to join you for your morning coffee or tea with fresh pastries and a great playlist.

Happy Hour at Home. If your home bar is already well stocked (see page 210), you'll likely just need to pick up a few mixers, or lemons, limes, and oranges for garnishes. This is a great way to host the after-work unwind, without the hefty bar tab.

Let's Find Out. Tell your friends to grab an ingredient from their fridge or pantry and come over. Together you can get creative to make a snack or meal with everyone's offerings.

Noodling & Doodling. Tell guests to bring their journals and their imaginations, and see where the afternoon takes you.

Pizza & Problem-Solving. When a friend or loved one is in need of some fresh perspective, invite a few trusted confidantes, order pizza, and spend the evening comparing ideas and brainstorming solutions.

Snack & Yap. Make a snack plate and talk in circles until it's empty.

Sweatpants Screenings. This is a perfect activity for a rainy day or a snowy afternoon. The dress code is "come as you are" and the menu is nothing fancy. Watch your favorite movie franchise or binge a guilty-pleasure reality TV show. Fill up on popcorn and pause frequently for chatter.

FOR LATE NIGHTS & EARLY MORNINGS

I love hosting when my favorite people are in town. If you are like me and your friends and family members live a bit farther away than the next town over, you might find yourself hosting guests who spend the night or a few nights with you (perhaps over a long weekend or during an extended holiday). You'll want to savor this time together, so let's establish some good hosting rituals for overnight guests.

A Checklist for Preparing to Host Overnight Guests

- ❑ Ask guests if they have allergies or dietary restrictions.
- ❑ Add their favorite things to your grocery list. For example, my dear friend Alexandria appreciates an herbal tea, so I pick up a few interesting tea options when I'm expecting her for a stay.
- ❑ Prepare your guest room or sleeping accommodations. Make sure you have fresh sheets, towels, and washcloths ready.
- ❑ Check and replenish toiletries, such as body wash, shampoo, conditioner, and body lotion. (You can find a more detailed list of toiletries for the guest bathroom on page 221.)
- ❑ Stock up on frequently forgotten items. I keep a small jar with new toothbrushes. I also have extra makeup remover wipes, floss picks, hygiene products, and phone chargers.

For the Nightstand

The spirit of hospitality is in the details. Think about the touches that have brought you comfort (and convenience) at your favorite hotels. You can draw inspiration from these experiences to make your guest accommodations feel extra special. I like to focus my welcome on the nightstand. I'll set it with:

- A vase of fresh lavender
- A water carafe and glasses (I like to add a sprig of rosemary)
- A snack (my favorites: veggie chips, edamame crisps, dark chocolate bark, macarons)
- A book of poetry or a favorite indie magazine
- An extra key (if the guest is staying for a few nights)
- A handwritten note with the Wi-Fi password

In the Morning

Despite my profession as an event planner, which frequently requires me to be a night owl, I am really a morning person, and I consider a communal breakfast to be very special bonding time. As the host, you'll get to help people start and set the tone for their day. So let's get these vibes right.

First and foremost, you'll want to ensure that you have coffee and tea, a selection of creamers and sweeteners, fresh juices, and fresh fruit. Make sure everything is intuitively placed and clearly labeled, so guests can help themselves as they roll out of bed and throughout their stay. From here, we build. Here are a few breakfast approaches to consider.

Easy Like Sunday Morning. Go with fresh bagels, biscuits, and breads (homemade or from the local bakery). Serve with an array of butters, cream cheeses, jams, and honey.

A Quick Start. Arrange a DIY parfait station with Greek yogurt, jam, fruit, and granola. This is ideal if you've got a full day's itinerary ahead or if guests will be departing that morning and you want to give them a nourishing send-off.

Brunch. If cooking a big bountiful late-morning breakfast is your vibe, perfect a few go-to dishes that you can make confidently. As you decide what will be on your brunch menu, strive for balance among protein, starch, and fruits and vegetables. On my list: a frittata with seasonal veggies, herbs, and feta; pancakes or French toast; and thick-cut bacon glazed with pure maple syrup, sprinkled with black pepper, and baked in a 400°F (200°C) oven for 15 to 20 minutes. As you master the techniques for *your* go-to items, you can explore seasonal variations and accompaniments to keep things interesting.

Simply Enjoying the Company. When the plan is to stay in your pajamas and spend the morning on the couch, deep in chatter, you cannot go wrong with an offering of coffee and coffee cake (see page 36).

Coffee Cake

Serves 12

Sweet but not too sweet, this versatile cake can be enjoyed with your morning coffee or served as an afternoon snack. The cake can be made the day before, and remains fresh in an airtight container at room temperature for up to 3 days.

CINNAMON SUGAR TOPPING

1 cup packed (220 g) dark brown sugar

¼ cup (50 g) granulated sugar

1½ teaspoons ground cinnamon

1 teaspoon ground nutmeg

½ teaspoon ground allspice

CAKE

Baking spray

2 cups (250 g) unbleached cake flour

1 teaspoon baking soda

1 teaspoon baking powder, preferably aluminum-free

½ teaspoon kosher salt

½ cup (1 stick/113 g) unsalted butter, at room temperature

1 cup (200 g) granulated sugar

1 teaspoon pure vanilla extract

2 large eggs, at room temperature

12 ounces (340 g) sour cream

Make the cinnamon sugar topping: In a small bowl, whisk together the brown sugar, granulated sugar, cinnamon, nutmeg, and allspice. Set aside.

Make the cake: Preheat the oven to 350°F (175°C). Coat a 9-inch (23 cm) round cake pan with baking spray.

In a medium bowl, whisk together the flour, baking soda, baking powder, and salt.

In the bowl of a stand mixer fitted with the paddle attachment (or in a large bowl using a handheld mixer), cream the butter and sugar together on medium speed until fluffy, about 3 minutes. Add the vanilla. Add the eggs one at a time, beating well after each addition until fully incorporated, about 30 seconds.

Reduce the mixer speed to medium-low. Add half the flour mixture to the butter mixture and mix until just combined. Add half the sour cream and mix until just combined. Repeat with the remaining flour mixture, then the remaining sour cream, until combined. Turn off the mixer and scrape down the sides of the bowl, making sure the batter is fully mixed.

Pour half the batter into the prepared pan; use an offset spatula to make sure the top is even. Sprinkle with half the cinnamon sugar topping. Spoon the remaining batter on top in an even layer. Sprinkle the remaining cinnamon sugar evenly on top.

Bake for about 50 minutes, until a toothpick inserted into the center of the cake comes out clean. Remove from the oven and let cool completely in the pan on a wire rack, about 1 hour. Invert onto a platter and serve.

Two

The Anatomy of a Good Shindig

Now that you are standing on a solid hosting foundation, we can build your skill set for planning parties, holidays, and other special get-togethers. In this section, I've combined the lessons I've learned professionally with the techniques I most use personally. We'll cover every convivial detail with a thoughtfulness that will lead to more interesting social gatherings.

Planning with Intention 40

What's Your (Party) Type? 42

Timing Is Everything 44

Finding Your Party People 47

Party Priorities 52

Visualizing Your Party 54

Food & Drinks 59

Atmosphere & Design 62

Music & Entertainment 68

Lists, Lists, Lists 77

The Art of Hosting 83

PLANNING WITH INTENTION

Whenever I am planning a party (both personally and professionally), I start by setting clear and specific intentions—the "why" for the party. Today's parties take place in a world that is deeply flawed, and that is sometimes hard, unfair, and unkind. Parties are our meeting place for hope, joy, and love amid feelings of loss, loneliness, and disappointment. Parties have the power to define cultures and reinforce community bonds, and they serve as symbols of belonging, leisure, and enjoyment. With this much potential in even the smallest of gatherings, hosts have an incredible opportunity to create spaces for people that can heal their hearts. To do so, we must anchor our events to an aim, goal, wish, or desire that we want to share with our guests.

When I started my supper club, I was in my early twenties, living in the city, and my friends and roommates there were in a constant state of hustle and bustle. Our schedules and social calendars were not always aligned for dinner, so eating alone was a frequent occurrence. This didn't sit well with me, and I wondered how many other young or single professionals were in the same boat. The *intention* for my dinner parties was to take a lonely Tuesday-night dinner and turn it into something special and momentous. I wanted guests to leave feeling seen, cared for, and a little more connected. Chasing this desire became the cornerstone of my party planning process.

At every step, I would ask myself how a particular detail would resonate with my guests and move them closer to the event's goal. When guests leaving my events would say, "Thank you; I needed this," I knew that the intentions of my party had resonated with them. To this day, I still find this to be one of the best compliments a guest can give me on their way out the door.

As someone who has attended more parties than I can count, I make intention setting my first order of business because I know that the absence of a well-defined intention is often what makes a party feel stale and uninspiring. Even when you are hosting a small and seemingly casual get-together, do not take this step for granted. Our time together is *always* precious.

When intention setting for your party, you have to go beyond the occasion (a birthday, a holiday, an accomplishment) and identify how you want to make people *feel*. Grab your entertaining journal and jot down the answers to the questions opposite. As you step further into the party planning process, returning to these answers can help focus (and simplify) the tasks ahead. Focused intentions will be the filter you use to help make decisions about the guest list, determine your priorities, stick to your budget, and stay calm and collected while hosting (because you will know that the party is about so much more than perfect execution).

Intention Setting

- What are you celebrating? What is the occasion?
- Why does the occasion matter to you and your potential guests?
- Why does this specific moment in time call for you to host the get-together?
- What is your aim, goal, desire, or wish for hosting this party?
- Why should people come? What social need will this party fulfill for them?
- What do you want guests to walk away feeling?

WHAT'S YOUR (PARTY) TYPE?

Deciding what type of party to host is your next big step in the planning process. This step comes after intention setting because you want to identify a party format that supports your goal and furthers your efforts to host parties that are meaningful, logistically reasonable, and unique. (That *is* why you are here, right?) I can't tell you how often a client or friend comes to me and says, "I want to host a dinner party." And when I ask why, they struggle to answer or begin telling me about an occasion, not an intention. They jump quickly into the "how"—the menu they want, their design ideas—showing me images they found on social media. In that moment, I know they are on a one-way trip to getting lost in the sauce. But this won't happen to you, dear reader, because your sauce is already seasoned with intention.

Let's review a few standard party types you have to choose from. Then I'll illustrate how each one can complement a specific party goal. (Later, in part 3, I'll show you examples of how I hosted each of these different party types.)

As you consider the type of party you want to host, you should reflect on the intentions you are setting for it. For example:

- If you want to spend the evening catching up and exchanging stories with old friends, you might host an intimate dinner party.
- If your goal is to get to know other parents in your neighborhood, you might host a community café, inviting everyone to stop by on a Saturday morning for a cup of coffee, a juice box, and fresh pastries before their afternoon errands and commitments.
- If you want to celebrate the history of your neighborhood or uplift local businesses, you might organize the annual block party.
- If you and your friends share a love of films and need more time for leisurely bonding, you might start hosting watch parties to enjoy new and old movies together.

Party Formats

TYPE	DESCRIPTION	EXAMPLES
Communal Meal	A seated party that is centered on guests enjoying a meal together.	Brunch Luncheon Dinner party
Mix and Mingle	A standing or lounge-style gathering where guests are encouraged to socialize or participate in various activities. Traditionally, food is served as passed appetizers and beverages are available at stations.	Café or tea party Cocktail party House party
Cookout or Block Party	An outdoor event, often on a holiday, where food is prepared on a grill and accompanied by lively music, dancing, games, and fellowship.	Memorial Day Juneteenth Fourth of July Labor Day
Activity-Based Gathering	An event that is organized around a specific hobby or interest.	Book club Craft party Game night Watch party

TIMING IS EVERYTHING

Time is a blessing. When you are planning for a party, the more time you have for the planning phase, the more interesting the experience will be. Whenever possible, try not to be in a rush; the best party plans are cooked low and slow.

Choose Your Event Date & Time

When determining the best date for the party, assuming it is not predetermined (like in the case of a holiday, a birthday, or a watch party for a live event), you want to give yourself enough time to plan and tend to all the details. Ideally, you want to have five to six weeks for a large or formal gathering, and three to four weeks for a more casual one. I find that this timeline gives me the space I need to move intentionally and think creatively. It sets a pace that makes it easy to fit in planning with the rest of my life's to-do lists while providing guests with sufficient notice as well.

Are there any holidays or community happenings that might conflict with your chosen event? If the party is outside, do you need a rain date, or is moving the party inside an option?

After you choose a date, you'll need to determine the party's start and end times. Typically, a casual event like a house party does not need to keep to a strict timeline, but as a host you should have a general sense of how you want the party to progress. For a dinner party on a weeknight, you might want to start the party at six o'clock, serving cocktails and light bites while you wait for all the guests to arrive. You may plan to sit for dinner around seven, serve dessert around eight, and anticipate the party "ending" around nine. This timeline will look very different from that for a Friday-night cocktail party or a Saturday cookout. For now, this timeline is just a place to start. Jot it down and revisit it as more ideas and details come together.

A Timeline for Planning

When your party's date and time is set, the timeline below can help guide you through the planning process. We'll cover all these steps in more detail in the pages that follow, but this chart will give you an idea of pacing for all the planning elements.

This is a starting point to keep the process flowing smoothly and at a pace that should feel more fun than stressful. As you begin to host more frequently, you will home in on a timeline that works best for you and your hosting style.

5 to 6 weeks before	Set an intention for your occasion (see page 40). Choose a party type, date, and time (see pages 42–45). Draft the guest list (see pages 47–51). Determine your priorities and budget (see pages 52–53). Get creative about your party's feeling, theme, and other special details (see pages 54–57).
4 weeks before	Send invitations (see page 50). Set a food and drinks menu (see pages 59–61). Make decisions about music and entertainment needs (see pages 68–74).
3 weeks before	Start shopping for necessary supplies, décor elements, favors, and other special touches.
2 weeks before	Confirm final RSVPs so you have an accurate head count and understanding of dietary restrictions or allergies. Restock nonperishable pantry items and pick up any desired wine, beer, or spirits. Make lists and work through the final planning details (see pages 77–81).
1 week before	Go through the Pre-Party Checklist on page 78.
Day of the party	Do your final setup, cooking, and preparation. Then enjoy the party!

FINDING YOUR PARTY PEOPLE

Having the right people at your party is key to ensuring that everyone feels safe to relax and have a good time. When a party feels stale or superficial, it is likely because the guests have not been properly considered and, as a result, no one is comfortable enough to really connect. I've already told you that I believe great parties can bring out the best in people, but that's only possible when party hosts truly understand what those people need.

I've found that the most fulfilling social experiences include people who have different perspectives, lifestyles, interests, and beliefs but are like-minded in a few important ways: They are kindhearted, open-minded, empathetic, and curious. At my parties, these qualities have always been the requirements for entry. Because let's be honest: Not everyone on your family tree is going to pass the vibe check, and tolerating their intolerance *is* a choice (a harmful one). The most important responsibility you have as host is to curate an environment where all your guests can thrive. So develop your guest list with care and discernment, and strive for a mix of people who will come willing to exchange ideas, embrace their commonalities, and explore their differences. On the following pages, I'll share the steps I take when I am in charge of the guest list.

A Step-by-Step Guest List Guide

1 Determine Your Capacity

First, you'll need to identify the number of people you can comfortably accommodate in your chosen entertaining space. You can use the formula below to determine your approximate capacity. This is an important first step because guests are more engaged when they have enough space to enjoy the party. Review the quirks of your space and how to create the best flow. Then factor in the type of party you want to host. If you are planning a seated dinner party or gathering, your capacity will have to align with the amount of seating at your dinner table or tables. If you are hosting a house party where guests will be standing and moving about, you'll need to ensure that they have enough space to eat, drink, talk, and dance. Adjust the capacity as needed. Write this final number down and keep it front of mind as you track RSVPs.

2 Make a First Draft

Write down the names of everyone you would want to invite. As you make this list, take into account whether the guest would be invited with a plus-one and if the party is going to be kid-friendly. Make note of couples and families as needed so you have an accurate count.

3 Narrow It Down

Once you have all the potential guests' names written down, take a look at this list with a more critical eye. Inviting too many guests can be detrimental to the experience and your budget. At first glance, you should look at the list with regard to

The Party Capacity Formula

The square footage of your designated entertaining area	−	The approximate square footage that will be occupied by larger event elements (e.g., the food table, the bar, other furniture, music setup)	÷	8 square feet

possible invitees' personalities, interests, hobbies, and life stages. Then ask yourself: Why is this person on the list? How will this person interact with the other guests on the list? Will these guests play well together? Continue to narrow down the names until you have a list that feels fitting and interesting.

4 Strategize Before You Send

Tally the number of people on your working list. How does this compare to the capacity you determined in step one? As a general guide, you can invite about 20 percent more guests than your ideal party size because some will be unable to attend. (That said, if it's a dinner party, I wouldn't exceed 20 percent because your table is a certain size and you truly can't risk too many confirmations at the beginning. But if it's a cookout, you might go as high as 30 percent more since people will be coming and going and the setup is more spacious.)

If your invite list far exceeds the number of people you can comfortably accommodate, create tiers within the list to prioritize the invitation strategy. Tier one is the people you definitely want to invite, and tier two is "invitees in waiting"—people you would really love to host but need to wait to invite until you've received a sufficient number of declines from those in tier one. This will help ensure that the number of confirmed guests does not get too far over capacity. If you need to take this tiered approach, try to start the invitation process one to two weeks earlier than normal, and set an initial RSVP date that is earlier, too, so you have enough time before the party date to invite and hear back from guests on the tier two list.

Disclaimer: The tiered approach is a delicate dance, and you must handle with care. Where possible, try to divide tier one and tier two lists by groups. Ideally people from the same social circle are in the same tier, to prevent someone in tier two from finding out about your party before you've had the opportunity to extend an invitation.

5 Design & Send the Invites

You are being incredibly thoughtful in planning this party. Your invitation will set the tone for the event. In design and language, invitations should align with the occasion and offer a preview of the party.

Ultimately, you want a guest's decision to attend to be as informed as your decision to invite them, so you'll want your invitation to be detailed. Alongside all the key party details, I like to share my intentions for the gathering and give guests a little insight on what or whom they can expect. Your guests may be invited to a lot of social engagements, so why (exactly) should they come to yours? For example, you might tell guests it is an "ice cream social for singles," from which guests will learn that there will be dessert *and* dating prospects. For another occasion, you might say, "Call your babysitter and save the date: We are hosting a playdate for parents." This tells your

Invitation Timing

When to send your invitations and when to set the RSVP date will vary based on the needs of your gathering and its formality. For example, if you're hosting a dinner party, you might base your RSVP date on how much time you will need to grocery shop (or, if you're hiring a caterer, on when they need to know the final guest count). For a craft party, you might want to give yourself enough time to order the necessary supplies. This chart will help you identify the right method and timeline for your invitations.

PARTY TYPE	PARTY STYLE	SUGGESTED INVITATION FORMAT	WHEN TO SEND INVITATIONS	WHEN TO REQUEST RSVPS
Communal Meal	Casual	Text	3 weeks before	1 week before
	Formal or special occasion	Digital invite or printed invitation	6 weeks before	2 weeks before
Mix and Mingle	Casual	Text message	4 weeks before	1 week before
	Formal or special occasion	Digital invite or printed invitation	6 weeks before	2 weeks before
Cookout or Block Party	Casual	Text message or digital invite	4 weeks before	1 week before
Activity-Based Gathering	Casual	Text message	4 weeks before	1 week before
	Formal or special occasion	Digital invite or printed invitation	6 weeks before	2 weeks before

friends who might be first-time parents that they can come over and meet others who understand the journey they are on. (Notice that this line also lets everyone know it is an adults-only get-together.) Making your intentions clear ensures that everyone RSVP'ing "yes" is on the same page. This is what will unlock the gathering magic.

A CHECKLIST FOR INVITATION DETAILS

- ❑ **The type of party** (e.g., a cookout or a cocktail party)
- ❑ **What guests can expect at this party** (e.g., a preview of your intentions for hosting)
- ❑ **The date and time**
- ❑ **The location**
- ❑ **The specifics.** Make clear if there is a dress code, a plus-one policy, a child policy, or any other special request so that guests can be prepared. If the event is a birthday gathering, wedding or baby shower, housewarming party, or other opportunity for celebration, it is also appropriate to include a registry or gifting guidance.
- ❑ **The RSVP date and requested information.** Depending on the details of the party, this might include dietary restrictions and allergies; accessibility needs; the name of their plus-one; what they'll be bringing to a potluck; or other fun details that will help you further customize the party (e.g., a favorite topping for the dessert bar or a baby photo for a guessing game).

Once you've landed on the wording for your invitations, you can create complementary graphics on websites like Canva or Etsy or make virtual invitations on platforms like Paperless Post or Partiful. If it is a more formal occasion, you can print invitations using services from websites like Minted.

6 Reflect on the Final Guest List

As you begin to receive RSVPs, revisit what you know about these guests. Different people will have different needs, and you must be prepared for both the social butterflies and the wallflowers. This last look at your guest list is where the poetry happens. The nuances you observe will help you decide if you need to send additional invites to bring a balance of personalities for any chance outliers.

Also take note of commonalities that can help you tailor your plans to the guests who are available to attend: Grab your entertaining journal and write down any particular interests, accommodations, or considerations for each guest that may become relevant as you begin outlining the structure and details of the party. Having a cognizance for people and what they need will be the magic of your hosting experience. You'll know more confidently what will delight your guests, what conversations will pique their interest, and whom they will enjoy sitting next to. With party planning (and in life), you will find your way once you find your people.

PARTY PRIORITIES

You cannot have it all (well, at least not at the same time). And the best hosts do not try to *do* it all. Our next step is to pinpoint your party priorities and set a budget that you will feel good about.

Identify What's Most Important to You

When you get into the planning of a party, you'll quickly realize that there are so many elements, it is easy to get overwhelmed. This is where the intention-setting exercise (see page 41) can help you stay grounded in what is really important. Another technique to employ is ranking your party priorities.

First, make a list of all the party elements that feel most important to you or for the occasion. This might include food, drinks, music, décor, entertainment, favors, and so on. Identify the three elements from this list that feel essential, and two or three that you'd deem least important. For example, I love food, so that is always my number one consideration. My number two is music, and depending on the occasion, my number three is usually favors or games. On the opposite side, typically ranking low on my list are fanciful décor and a large number of bar offerings. How you prioritize a party's elements should help guide both your energy and your spending. If you are throwing the party for someone else (e.g., a birthday, anniversary, or accomplishment), complete this exercise while keeping *their* priorities front and center, to ensure that the party is true to them as the guest of honor.

Setting a Budget

Now that you've got your priorities in order, it's time to talk about the budget. Determine the amount of money you feel comfortable investing in the party. A house party budget includes food, beverages, music, entertainment, décor, sometimes favors, and often home essentials to clean, host, and clean again.

When you are deciding where to spend and where to save, revisit the intentions of the party and your priorities. Below is a reference for how a party budget typically takes shape. Of course, this will vary based on the occasion, the type of party, and your personal hosting style. You can use this as a general guide and eliminate anything that does not serve the occasion or more casual hosting. The most important thing I want you to take away here is being intentional with your spending. Set a budget and stick to it, so you can feel good about hosting and hosting more often.

GUIDING YOUR SPENDING

Food and beverage	30%
Décor, flowers, paper goods (printed menus, signage, or other custom details), or rentals *(if necessary)*	25%
Music and entertainment *(if necessary)*	10%
Special touches like favors, or other customized details *(if desired)*	10%
Home essentials (e.g., cleaning products or guest toiletries) and party-specific supplies	10%
Contingency fund (for unexpected needs)	15%

VISUALIZING YOUR PARTY

I've always viewed party planning as an act that requires both sides of your brain. You need your "left brain" (generally associated with logic and reason) and your "right brain" (known for creativity). In this regard, you might consider everything we've done up until this step to be the left brain of party planning. And now it is time to rev up that right brain power to imagine how the party will look and feel.

Give the Party a Feeling Statement

I like to create a feeling statement for my parties to guide my approach to all the details. The role of the feeling statement is to describe the vibe and serve as your North Star as you start to creatively construct the party. For more casual gatherings, your feeling statement might remain unspoken. For other occasions, the feeling statement might be connected to a more overt party theme. Some examples:

- I want the party to feel like a Caribbean vacation.
- I want the party to feel like a girls' night at a lavish hotel.
- I want the party to feel like a prom night in the '90s.

These feeling statements should give you a creative foundation to build on. The "Caribbean vacation" is going to have a very different menu, dress code, atmosphere, and playlist than a "'90s prom night." So grab your entertaining journal and finish this sentence:

I want my party to feel like . . .

Make a Mood Board

Once you've arrived at the right feeling statement, you can start your party's mood board. This is a collection of images, colors, patterns, and words or phrases that capture the desired style of the event. It should include food, beverages, décor, paper goods, and other details that you are excited about for the particular occasion. The mood board is where the personality of the event is defined. As you start making choices about the menu, styling flowers, and shopping for decorations or favors, you should refer to this mood board to make sure every element complements the others. If you decide to hire an event services provider for food, decorations, or floral arrangements, it will also help you communicate your vision and ensure that everyone is on the same page. To make your mood board, you can use an online generator like Pinterest, or approach it scrapbook-style with cutouts from magazines and newspapers.

Add Spectacular Details

While your creative juices are flowing, I have one more tip for you: Focus on the small and add something spectacular. I believe the magic of an event is often in the details. As you plan to host, be on the lookout for the small gestures that will make guests feel special. This might be handwritten notes, or thoughtfully sourced favors (see page 218 for inspiration), or your attentiveness to the guests' dietary concerns. It is often these choices that will distinguish how you host from how others do.

At the same time, I also like to have just one element that is a bit of a spectacle to grab guests' attention and give them something to remember. This can be whatever you want it to be: a fancy welcome cocktail; a gorgeous, oversize floral arrangement for guests to happen upon in the kitchen; a beautifully plated dish like a whole fish that you bring out on a fanciful serving platter; a dessert that you finish with a blowtorch tableside just before serving; or a surprise performance after dinner. You get the picture. Be creative with this. Even when you are hosting a more casual gathering, you should still look for one small way to grab guests' attention. These moments are often best placed toward the beginning or end of the festivities because guests always remember their first impression of an event and their last one.

Red pepper
99¢ LB

FOOD & DRINKS

In planning dinner parties for a living, I've developed a clear philosophy regarding party food: There should be plenty, and it should be *really* good.

Plan Your Menu

You have lots of delicious decisions to make when it comes to your party's menu and how exactly the food and beverages will get to the table.

What do you want to serve? It is always best to start with foods and flavors that excite you as the host. When you cook or serve things that you personally love, chances are guests will love them, too.

Are your menu ideas practical for the party you are hosting? Once you have your initial ideas, consider how you might need to adapt them to work for your party's type, size, and format. In doing so, you might realize that the menu ideas you love require a little creativity to work for the party you are hosting. For example, chicken and waffles is a great party dish, but how you serve this dish at a seated brunch for four people will look very different from how it would be served at a cocktail party for forty. Throughout the party planning process, you will be doing a delicate dance between idea and execution. Don't shy away from this work—embrace it. You will have a better party because of it.

What is the temperature? Consider both the weather and where the food will be served (inside or outside?). Personally, I enjoy ice cream any time of year, but a hot chocolate bar may be a better choice when the temperature drops down low. If the party is inside on a crisp fall day with a mild temperature, you might want to offer hearty salads, artisanal breads, and braised meats. If the party is outside on a hot summer day, I'd skip the cheese board and the three-layer cake with buttercream frosting.

What ingredients are in season and/or locally available? Shopping in sync with nature will ensure that you have the best and most sustainably sourced ingredients contributing to your menu. When possible, go to your local farmers' markets, butchers, fishmongers, and bakeries to learn, shop, and find inspiration. Simply knowing where to find the *best* ingredients available will help your menu to shine.

What are your guests' needs? Always request info about dietary restrictions and allergies during the RSVP process to ensure that you have something for everyone. Nothing is worse than when a guest comes to your party and there is nothing for them to eat.

Start Cooking or Start Delegating

Now that you have a vision for the menu, you must determine how you will get this food to the table. Spoiler alert: I'll never tell you that you have to make everything yourself (or from scratch) in order to be the host with the most. We've got options! You can:

Cook the food yourself if you enjoy cooking and feel confident preparing the dishes on your ideal menu. In this scenario, I opt for dishes that can be cooked and prepped in advance—I never want to be standing at the stove come party time. This is key to ensuring that you can be a present and participatory host when the party starts. *If you plan to cook or prepare the food and drinks yourself, check out page 208 for serving-size guidance.*

Make the event a potluck so guests share the responsibility of the menu and you save money in the process. A potluck-style menu plan is particularly useful for casual gatherings, holidays celebrations, and large cookouts. Potlucks typically work best when the participants share a familiarity or level of comfort with each other. Depending on the occasion, potlucks also work more smoothly when you establish a menu theme, or create a category-based sign-up list so you don't end up with three sides of potato salad and no desserts. *If you plan to host a potluck, check out page 155 for inspiration.*

Outsource the food preparation when you want to host but don't want the responsibility of cooking. You can order takeout for casual occasions or hire a chef or caterer for more formal ones—this route is particularly useful if you have a few menu ideas that fall outside your culinary confidence zone (or if cooking in general is just not your ministry!). *If you plan to hire help, check out page 214 for a guide to booking a private chef or caterer.*

Offer a Variety of Beverages

As with your food menu, you want to ensure that your drinks menu has something for everyone, including alcoholic, low-alcohol, and no-alcohol options (see the guide below). Set up a beverage station so guests can choose something without having to explain their preferences around alcohol to you or the group.

Knowing how to make a classic cocktail is a great party trick—see pages 212–213 for a few recipes. If you need help stocking your bar cart, see page 210. When it comes to mocktails, you want these to be as interesting and thoughtful in presentation as your cocktails. Don't treat them like an afterthought!

For large groups, consider making prebatched mocktails and cocktails so you don't get stuck playing bartender all night. If you prefer to hire a caterer or bar service to handle the beverages, see page 214 for guidance.

Boozy: Think martinis, margaritas, daiquiris, and juleps.

Less Boozy: A selection of beers, wines, and aperitifs.

Not Boozy: Water (still and sparkling), plus two or three additional options such as mocktails, fresh juices, sodas, coffee, and tea.

ATMOSPHERE & DESIGN

In this phase, we will bring your mood board to life and create visual interest through how you arrange your hosting environment and décor.

Find Your Flow

Whether you have a small entertaining space or a large one, when deciding how to set it up, it is important to consider how people will flow and where they will congregate. Imagine how guests will journey from the entrance to the points of engagement—from removing their shoes or their coats at the door to making their way to a welcome table with appetizers or to the bar and beyond. Guests tend to gather around the appetizers, in the kitchen, and at the bar, so putting some distance between these areas will prevent traffic jams. As you mentally (and perhaps literally) flow through your entertaining space, note adjustments that will need to be made for the party setup, such as furniture that might need to be rotated, tucked away, or added. In your entertaining journal, you can sketch out your floor plan and start a list of possible purchases or party rentals. (For guidance on party rentals, see page 214.)

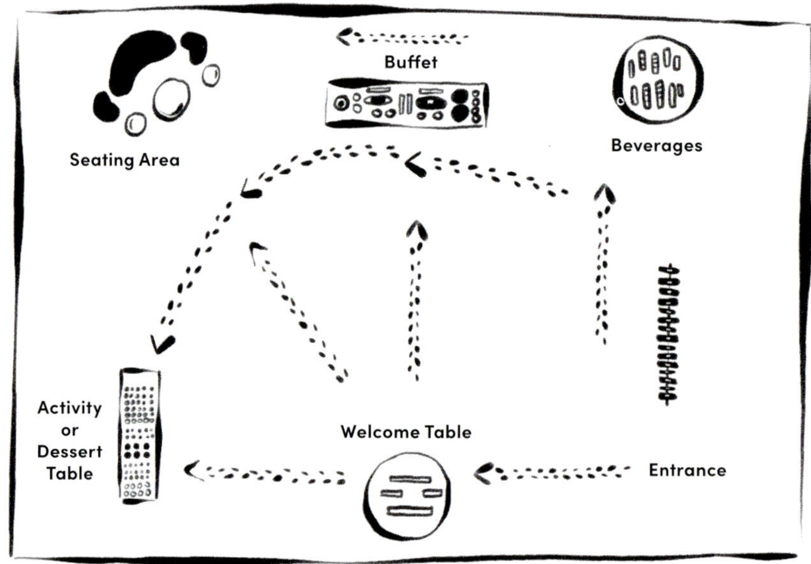

Control the Light

Practically, lighting will help people navigate the space, and it should be used strategically, to brighten pathways, hallways, and food or beverage tables. At the same time, lighting can complement the design of the party and contribute to its ambiance. Bright lighting and sun-drenched spaces will spotlight your décor choices and encourage high energy. Soft, dim lighting and candlelight will gently accent your décor choices and promote a more relaxed energy. Extremely low-lit or dark spaces with colorful or concentrated lighting will communicate mystery and excitement. Light can also be used to add color or to reinforce a party's feeling statement. Party themes like a candlelit soirée, dinner at the disco, or glowing after dark all demand specific lighting choices.

For most occasions, natural light for a daytime gathering and soft, warm light in the evening will be pleasing for guests. In the evening, be sure to employ dimmers if you have them; otherwise, consider using accent lamps, wall sconces, candles, string lights, and other decorative lighting to illuminate your entertaining space without turning on harsh overhead lights. For outdoor events, use twinkle lights, candles, illuminated spheres, lanterns, and outdoor floor lamps to brighten pathways, tables, and seating areas.

Be Intentional with Color

As with lighting, color choices can be indicative of a party's mood or personality. The science of color has been studied for centuries—and the influence of color on human perception and mood is debated across psychology, medicine, marketing, interior design, and even the culinary arts. From our earliest stages of childhood development, we've experienced color in relation to emotions. Recall watching characters in your Saturday-morning cartoons change colors to express feelings of anger, sickness, and love. It's the same reason why "seeing red" and "feeling blue" are phrases many of us can understand.

By recognizing the associative power that color can have on people, you can use it symbolically or to elicit the right emotions. Below, I've provided some examples of what certain colors are felt to convey that are common across studies and cultures, so you can play with color choices more intentionally at your next party.

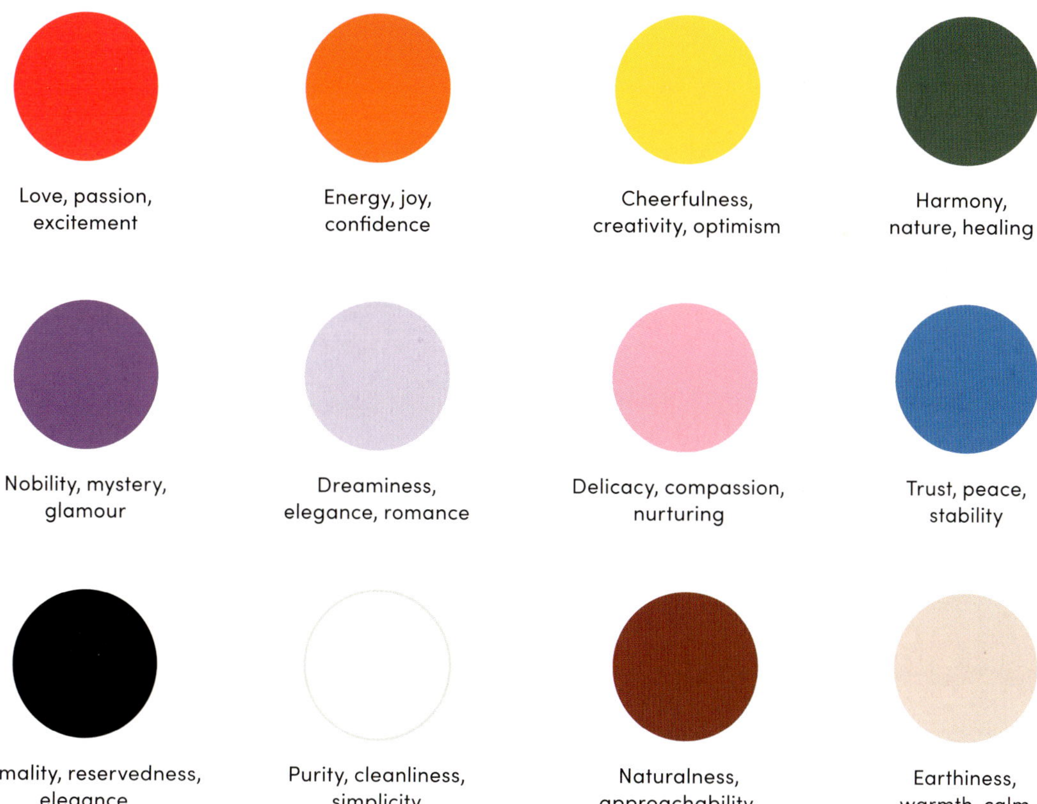

PRO TIPS

Party Décor

- **Do less, abundantly.** As a guest, it can be very flattering to see how much effort went into the preparations for your visit. But this does not mean that as the host, you have to do it *all* when it comes to decorations, nor do you have to be overly fancy or flashy. You can still delight your guests with one focal detail. For example, you can create a welcome arch with just balloons (instead of ballons *and* flowers). You can style your table with just candles (instead of candles *and* centerpieces). This is an especially useful principle when you don't want to spread your budget or energy across multiple décor elements. Instead, choose one and do it well. (This is a great tip for menu development as well.)
- **Play with texture and contrast.** Layering different surfaces, materials, and patterns will bring visual interest to your event design. For example, the color and texture of your dinner menu will pop more when the menu is on top of a patterned napkin and smooth stoneware.
- **Know when to use height.** Avoid floral arrangements or centerpieces that are too tall to see over at the dinner table, but use risers, ramekins, and cake stands to add different levels to your food display on a buffet table.
- **Embrace the unusual.** This will help spark conversation among guests. Instead of defaulting to flower arrangements, get creative with fruits, vegetables, potted plants, or branches. Integrate photographs, art, or poetry into your table design. Use items sourced from your pantry, forage in your backyard, or go thrifting for favors or other styling elements.
- **Don't disregard practicality.** Make design decisions that do not negatively affect the guest experience. Choose the serving ware option that is best for your menu—not just the one that is your preferred style. Go with the seating arrangement that is more comfortable and spacious for guests.

MUSIC & ENTERTAINMENT

The shared experience of music and the bonds formed through conversation, games, and activities will make your hosting endeavors more enjoyable for you and your guests.

Curate the Sound

Champagne corks popping, glasses clinking, silverware and stoneware exchanging gentle kisses, laughter floating above our favorite tunes—the sounds of a party have such a powerful effect on the event's energy. Recognizing this starts with acknowledging the effect that music can have on humans more generally. Music is known to reduce anxiety, lower blood pressure, and alleviate pain while improving mood, mental alertness, and memory. Hearing an old or familiar song releases dopamine, while listening to new music can stimulate memory and information processing. I gravitate toward older and more familiar song selections when I want guests to get up and dance or sing along. When it's time for guests to focus on the conversation, I'll opt for lo-fi sounds and sprinkle in a healthy dose of new music. As you curate your party's music, consider how your music choices will influence the energy you want to bring to the environment.

When deciding how to approach the music at your party, you can create a playlist on Spotify or hire musicians or a DJ. The right option for you will be evident from your party type, priorities, and budget. For a casual communal meal or an activity-based party, a playlist is likely all you need. However, if the occasion is a milestone celebration and you or the guest of honor really love music, then you might opt for a live performance. And if you are hosting a dance party or a cookout, a DJ might be at the top of your priorities list. If you decide to hire musicians or a DJ, check out page 215 for best practices and booking advice.

Reminder: Not Everyone Loves the Sounds of a Party

It is important to be considerate of your neighbors. If you are hosting more than twelve people or your event is running past 9 p.m., it is a good practice to inform any nearby neighbors that you will be hosting a party and to ask them to call or text you if the noise becomes a disturbance. After midnight, reduce the volume of amplified sound by 50 percent. This is also a good time to switch up the genre and tempo of the music to help the party wind down.

PRO TIPS

Building a Playlist

- **Incorporate a theme and a story.** Add songs to your playlist based on what you enjoy and the feelings you want to evoke in your guests. Genres like disco, hip-hop, R & B, Afrobeat, and sing-along-worthy songs will naturally make people loosen up.
- **Order the playlist to be like a roller coaster.** Start with mid-tempo or instrumental selections to build up the energy as guests arrive. The middle of the playlist should be filled with your favorite selections of popular music and old favorites. Then gradually slow the tempo to naturally bring the party to a close.
- **Consider your crowd.** As with all elements of the planning process, let your guests be your guide. It can be fun to ask guests to RSVP with a favorite song or a song request, so they can be part of the playlist-making experience. Or if you have a musically inclined friend or family member, share the playlist and party details with them and ask for their feedback or song suggestions.
- **Add extra songs.** I recommend including two extra hours of music. The first hour should be a collection of songs that you can enjoy before guests arrive—it will help ease the pre-party nerves as you finish prepping (cue the dance party for one). The last hour gives you a little extra wiggle room in case the party goes longer than expected. These songs can help wind the party down and get you through cleanup.
- **Make a playlist even if you plan to hire a musician or DJ.** The playlist can serve as backup if there are technical difficulties, for when musicians are taking a break, or if the party goes well past the service times for your booking.

Conversation Starters

Over the years of dining with friends and strangers, I've tested a *lot* of conversation starters and kept a record of all the questions that have led to the best tableside banter. I've compiled them for you here. You can turn to these questions when you need to start the dialogue during dinner, when you need the conversation to make an artful pivot, or when you find yourself in social settings where people are in need of prompts to begin engaging with each other. Test these questions out and make note of the ones that work for you and your guests.

FOR LIGHT DISCOVERY

- What is your favorite meal and why?
- What song is the soundtrack for your life right now?
- What is the first thing you do in the morning and the last thing you do at night?
- What type of media (music, books, TV, film, etc.) do you enjoy?
- What song do you dance to when no one is watching?
- What is one thing you can't live without?
- What do you wish you had more time for?
- What is your favorite family tradition?
- What travel destinations are on your bucket list right now?
- When you visit a new place, what do you do first?
- What was the last new thing you tried? How did it go?
- What is a new activity or hobby you want to try?
- What do you like to do on a leisurely weekend?
- What were you serious about as a child (e.g., hobbies, interests, fictional characters) that is now funny to you as an adult?
- If you could live in any movie or TV show universe for a year, which one would it be?

FOR GOING DEEPER

- How are you *really* feeling?
- How are you taking care of yourself in this season?
- What is your favorite thing about yourself?
- How do you like to express yourself?
- When do you feel most connected to others, your culture, or the world around you?
- What is an experience that taught you the most about yourself, life, or love?
- What is a life lesson that you've learned recently?
- What has success taught you? What has failure taught you?
- What's a memory that you want to go back and relive?
- How would you describe your life ten years ago? How would you describe your life now? And how do you hope to be able to describe your life ten years from now?
- What would you tell your younger self?
- What has been the most memorable moment of your life so far?
- How are you staying curious or feeding your curiosities right now?
- With plenty of money, no fear, and zero guilt, what would you do with your life?

FOR COMMUNITY GROWTH

- What is a change you've made recently that has improved your life for the better?
- What is a goal you are working toward right now?
- What are you most passionate about and why?
- What motivates you?
- What are you in need of most right now (e.g., time, resources, companionship)?
- What is the best advice you have ever received or some great advice you have received lately?
- What challenge are you working to overcome right now?
- What media (music, books, TV shows, films, etc.) do you recommend to the group and why?
- What do you think will be your legacy, or how do you wish to be remembered?
- What social issue are you most tuned in to and what resources do you recommend for others interested in the topic?
- What is something you can pour into others right now? And what do you need others to pour into you right now?
- Who is someone you admire that the rest of us should know about? (And why?)
- What word or mantra is guiding you right now?
- In what areas of your life are you feeling wiser? And in what areas are you looking to grow?
- What do you believe is the gift you want to share with this world?

FOR CELEBRATORY OCCASIONS

- What brings you the most joy?
- What is something that always makes you laugh?
- What is your favorite thing about this season of your life?
- What are you grateful for at this moment?
- What are you excited about right now?
- What is something you are looking forward to?
- What is some good news you've received recently?
- What were the small victories you savored this week?
- How do you like to celebrate your wins?
- What is something you're proud of yourself for doing?
- What is something your younger self would be proud of you for doing?
- What is a song that always gets you in the mood to dance?
- What is your go-to celebration meal or treat or indulgence?
- Do you have a celebration ritual?
- What has been inspiring to you lately?

Games & Activities

I believe a party should be all fun and games. Here is a list of ideas to employ as you host.

For After Dinner	Charades Board games (grab your favorites from your party pantry—in mine, you can find playing cards, backgammon, UNO!, dominoes, trivia games, Tapple, Settlers of Catan, Taboo, and more) Karaoke Trivia contests
For Special Occasions	Artist for live portraits and paintings Advice or recipe exchange Comedian DIY party favors (this one can work for kids' parties, too) Poetry performance Wine and/or cheese tasting
For Kids' Parties	Ball pit or bouncy castle Coloring station Face painting or temporary tattoos Magic show or science demonstration (this can work for adult parties, too) Professional storyteller Scavenger hunt

If hiring professional services, artists, or instructors feels fitting for your party, check out page 215 for best practices and booking advice.

TO DO LIST
order cakes

LISTS, LISTS, LISTS

Over the years, I've developed a love for lists, and in this phase, I hope you will find a healthy appreciation for them, too. Now that you are in the home stretch of the party planning, it's all about crossing your *t*'s and dotting your *i*'s. Use the list templates for guidance as you jot down your own lists in your entertaining journal.

Checklist for the Guest Experience

When we assume the responsibility of a host, our ultimate goal is to create an environment where everyone is comfortable enough to have a good time and really connect. And nothing ruins a party atmosphere more than when guests are hungry, hot, or otherwise uncomfortable. Below is a checklist to make sure you have considered all the party details that will make it easy for your guests to settle in.

- ❏ Does your menu accommodate the dietary needs and beverage preferences of all your guests?
- ❏ How is the weather? Do any additional accommodations need to be made for guests' comfort?
- ❏ If the party has a seated portion, have you assigned seats to ensure that everyone has a place? (For more on crafting seating charts, see page 161.) Similarly, if your activity requires pairs or your game night requires teams, make sure everyone is accounted for.
- ❏ Have you clearly communicated dress code requirements or other party-specific expectations so guests arrive confidently?
- ❏ If the party is kid-friendly, have you considered the safety of your entertaining space? Depending on the expected ages, review things like access to outlets, open flames or hot surfaces, pool safety, and separation of alcoholic beverages.

The Pre-Party Checklist

This should be an all-inclusive list of what you want to complete in the one to two weeks leading up to the party. The length and complexity of this list will vary based on the nature of the party and how much décor and cooking you plan to handle personally. Having a detailed pre-party to-do list has saved me on many occasions. Depending on the party type and your hosting style, this checklist might include to-dos like:

- ❏ **Check your party pantry and take inventory of your hosting essentials.** You should also check your bar cart to take inventory of wine, spirits, and mixers. Make sure you have everything you need, and start a list of anything that needs to be restocked or replaced.
- ❏ **Begin shopping for nonperishable items,** such as partyware (including any theme-related décor or customized party elements), toiletries, cleaning supplies, and other household necessities. (See page 221 for a list of toiletries that guests will appreciate.)
- ❏ **Finish the playlist** and give it a test listen—is anything missing?
- ❏ **Follow up with any hired businesses or local service providers** to confirm your final orders, arrival times, and final payments.
- ❏ **Prepare a clean slate.** A detailed checklist for pre-party cleaning is on pages 80–81. Remember to declutter the coat closet (for good presentation and extra storage) and clear out the refrigerator before you go shopping. This will be particularly useful for the freezer to ensure that you have plenty of storage space for ice.
- ❏ **Start to grocery shop.** When developing your grocery list, organize it based on the layout of your grocery store or farmers' market so you can shop more efficiently. Choose shopping date(s) throughout the week based on the menu and when you can pick up the freshest ingredients from your market or specialty purveyors. When you return home, use colorful sticky notes to quickly identify ingredients for corresponding recipes or courses.

cornbread
salad
STAUB
mac & cheese
lamb chops
STAUB
rice
green beans
gravy
mini tarts
chicken

The Final Prep Timeline

This timeline for the day (and day before) will vary based on the type of party you are hosting, its complexity, and whether you will have any support with meal preparation or setup, but the below is a good starting point that you can adapt based on your needs. When I am doing a lot of cooking or decorating for the occasion, I'll also include time stamps for each task—so I can keep track of my pace and ensure that I'm ready to party on time.

THE DAY BEFORE

- ❑ Pick up fresh flowers and make arrangements.
- ❑ Start baking, prepping, or marinating as required by your menu.
- ❑ Set up or rearrange furniture as needed, tucking away anything fragile or hard to replace if hosting a large or kid-friendly get-together.
- ❑ Take out serving platters, bowls, serving utensils, beverage carafes, and buckets. Clean them and label them with sticky notes so you know which dishes and drinks will go in each.
- ❑ Clean glasses, plates, and utensils that may have been collecting dust between gatherings.
- ❑ Set the table, welcome table, and bar. If applicable, steam linen tablecloths and napkins. Arrange all party décor as necessary.

THE MORNING OF

- ❑ Continue baking, prepping, or marinating as required by your menu.
- ❑ Send a brief text or email to your guests. The note should include a reminder of the time, the address, the dress code, and any relevant information for their arrival (e.g., "Please park in the back" or "Our door is the one on the left with the balloon").
- ❑ Ensure that the bathroom(s) guests will be using are stocked with soap, lotion, toilet paper, hand towels, and toiletries. You should also remove trash and disinfect surfaces. Include a small vase of a fragrant flower like gardenia or lavender on the counter, or light a fragrant candle or turn on a diffuser.
- ❑ Vacuum all areas, lint roll all upholstered furniture, and wipe down surfaces one more time.

A FEW HOURS BEFORE

- ❏ If you're hosting indoors, open the windows and let a little fresh air into your space (weather permitting). You also want to cool down your space to a temperature that will feel comfortable once the room fills up. Typically, I turn down the thermostat 5 to 10 degrees depending on the party size and season, and adjust based on any feedback.
- ❏ Chill the beverages.
- ❏ Take a break from prep and get dressed.

THE HOUR BEFORE

- ❏ Finish food and beverage prep—filling ice buckets, slicing garnishes, setting the welcome table with appetizers and beverages.
- ❏ Close the doors to any rooms you do not want guests in.
- ❏ Just before guests arrive, replace the kitchen trash bag. You should also start the party with an empty sink, dish rack, and dishwasher, so dishes have a place to pile up or the dishwasher can be discreetly loaded as the night progresses.
- ❏ Set your lighting, start the playlist, and put the finishing touches on everything.
- ❏ Take a deep breath. The hard work is done. Be present and enjoy the party.

THE ART OF HOSTING

Being a great host is about so much more than being a great cook or having a great sense of home décor. When guests are in your space and under your care, how you make them feel will be the true measure of your role as host. I've learned that guests will feed off your energy—so it's time to loosen your grip on the plan and let the party flow. You should be the first to make a toast and the last to say goodnight. Below are my tips for being a more artful host.

Be present. You've done all the hard work to plan and prepare for hosting, and you deserve to enjoy the party, too. Put down your phone, mingle with your guests, enjoy the food, have a drink, laugh, and dance! When the host is present and at ease, guests will follow their lead.

Make strong introductions. When the party is in motion, it is important to help your guests settle into the space, which includes getting comfortable with the other guests. Most hosts will make introductions based on how people are connected to them. This may leave people feeling like the only thing they have in common is being friends with the host. Instead, try to include a few details that they have in common with each other, like similar hobbies, interests, travel plans, family compositions, and so on. This will give them a solid starting place for conversation. If you do this well, you will be able to slip away unnoticed and their conversation can extend far beyond small talk.

Give a memorable opening toast. An opening toast should be three things: brief, focused, and bubbling with gratitude. Include stories that will tug at guests' heartstrings or give them a good laugh. You might also share a quote or fun fact that will encourage deeper conversations throughout the evening. Ultimately, the goal of your opening toast is to make guests feel a sense of camaraderie and hope for what the rest of the party will bring. Remember to be yourself, be sincere, and have fun with it. I recommend writing down your opening toast in advance. You don't have to read it word for word, but the exercise will help you remember the points you want to hit.

Prepare to prompt. Whether the party is a communal meal or a mix and mingle, you should have a few conversation starters to help spark meaningful connections or break the ice (you can find some example questions on pages 71–73). In some cases, you'll just keep these tucked in your metaphorical back pocket. For larger gatherings, you might want to be more forward, adding prompts to the dinner menu, on cocktail napkins, or in small bowls at tables, allowing guests to use them at their discretion.

Help connect the dots. You put a lot of thought into arranging the party. Don't be afraid to share a few fun anecdotes or things you learned from the planning process. Did you discover a vintage shop in a neighboring town? Did you experiment with a new cooking technique? Did you venture to a new bakery? Sharing these details, which are usually kept behind the curtain, will make guests feel more invested in how it all comes together.

Don't sweat a spill, splash, or smash. As a general rule of thumb, anything that is valuable or irreplaceable should be removed from your entertaining space. Everything that remains in the space should be durable or easily replaceable. If an accident happens, guests will feel bad enough, so do your best to laugh it off and assure them that it is an easy cleanup. For this to be true, make sure to keep a few things handy: (1) paper towels and extra dish towels for a spill; (2) club soda and salt for a clothing stain; (3) a stronger stain remover like Wine Away or OxiClean; and (4) a broom and dustpan for a quick sweep.

Know how to wind the party down. You want the party to have a natural closing, rather than an abrupt end. Start by rolling out a cart with dessert, coffee, tea, or some infused water, whatever feels fitting for your occasion. In serving dessert, take the opportunity to thank everyone for being part of the festivities. Gradually start to lower the music, and bring in a bit more light. If offering party favors, make sure they are conveniently placed at the door or start to distribute them. Ultimately, you want to send guests off as gracefully as you received them.

Send thank-you notes. Guests will likely bring a thank-you gift or send a thank-you note to the host, but hosts can (and should) send a few thank-you notes, too. To guests, it can be a next-day text or email that communicates that you valued their company and contribution to the gathering. For hired service providers, it is nice to send a thank-you message—digital or handwritten. These notes will mean a lot.

The After Party

After all the late-night giggles are gone, the dishes are in the dishwasher, and the trash has been taken out, it's time to wind down and reflect. Grab your entertaining journal and write down your thoughts. What went well? What didn't go so well? What did you learn? What brought you joy? What will you remember? Collecting these thoughts and tidbits while the memories are still fresh in your mind is a great practice. When it's time to host again, you can return to these journal entries for insight and inspiration.

Help!

Here are the answers to the most common dilemmas hosting enthusiasts send my way.

Guests keep asking me what to bring! Even when you insist that you need absolutely nothing, guests typically don't like to show up empty-handed. If it is a casual gathering, recommend a contribution to the meal, like a beverage or a dessert. If it is a special occasion, you might say, "Gifts are not necessary, but if you insist, I'd never turn down a [*insert three or four of your favorite things*]."

Nothing is going according to my plan! When things go wrong or don't go exactly to plan, remember that this is the excitement of hosting. If you need a moment to reset, step outside or into a private room to regain your composure. No matter how upset or disappointed you may be, taking time out for a few deep breaths is important so you can stay calm, think on your feet, resolve the matter quickly, and resume having a good time.

A guest showed up with a plus-one that I was not expecting! Even with a clearly communicated plus-one policy and an RSVP date, sometimes an extra guest (or two) will wind up at your door. When that happens, be as gracious and accommodating as you can.

The conversation is taking a turn! It happens. People can be unpredictable. When you need to redirect a conversation that is feeling distasteful, you have two options. Transition the conversation with a new topic: "Speaking of . . ." or "Before I forget . . ." Or end the conversation by attending to the needs of the party: "Pardon me, my hosting duties call." Or "Please excuse the abrupt transition, but it's time for . . ."

It's getting a bit messy! You can clean as you go, but be discreet. You don't want guests to take this as a cue to leave. Place abandoned glasses and plates in the sink or dishwasher. At the end of the night, if guests insist on helping you clean up, let them help pack up leftovers and pile up dishes. Save the trash collecting, dishwashing, counter cleaning, and sweeping for after the guests leave.

They are not ready to drive! With late-night parties, especially cocktail parties, keep an eye out for guests who have been doing a bit more imbibing, and make sure they are not intending to drive. Help arrange a trusted car ride home and keep extra pillows, blankets, and pajamas in a nearby closet to easily accommodate a couch guest or two.

three

Parties at My Place

By now I hope you are feeling empowered to start planning and hosting events of your own. In this section, I will give you an inside look at a few of my parties to see how the tips and techniques from the previous sections come together when I am hosting. As you flip through these pages, keep an eye out for ideas, how-tos, and recipes that you can remix and reimagine for your own events.

Sunday Supper 89

Crafts & Crudités 111

The Cookout 125

Playtime & Provisions 141

Friendsgiving Potluck 155

Grown Kid's Birthday Party 175

Hope & Midnight 189

SEASON:
Spring

GUEST COUNT:
6

PLANNING TIME:
4 weeks

Sunday Supper

FOR A BOOST OF CAMARADERIE

There is power in passing plates. Research has found that those who eat socially more often than they eat alone feel happier and have higher rates of resilience and self-esteem. Mastering the art of a small dinner party was the first step in my hosting journey, so it is only right that we start here, too.

The goal for this gathering was to break from routine and spend time with friends. I wanted the experience to be low-fuss, allowing us to really be present before diving back into the demands of work and life.

When I'm hosting, I like to remind guests that you can't fake it at a dinner party. You're going to sit next to someone for over an hour, so you are destined to become friends or spirited debaters, and if neither, it's going to be terribly awkward. A successful dinner party requires everyone's active participation. It is not one of those social gatherings that you can attend and hide behind your phone before sneaking out early. If you want to experience the magic of a dinner party, everyone has to be open, curious, and willing to be a little vulnerable. For this dinner, I invited guests from different social circles—a combination of new friends, old friends, coworkers, and neighbors. Mixing up the guest list gives everyone the comfort of familiarity and the stimulation of the unknown. I consider this the perfect mix for making dinner parties interesting.

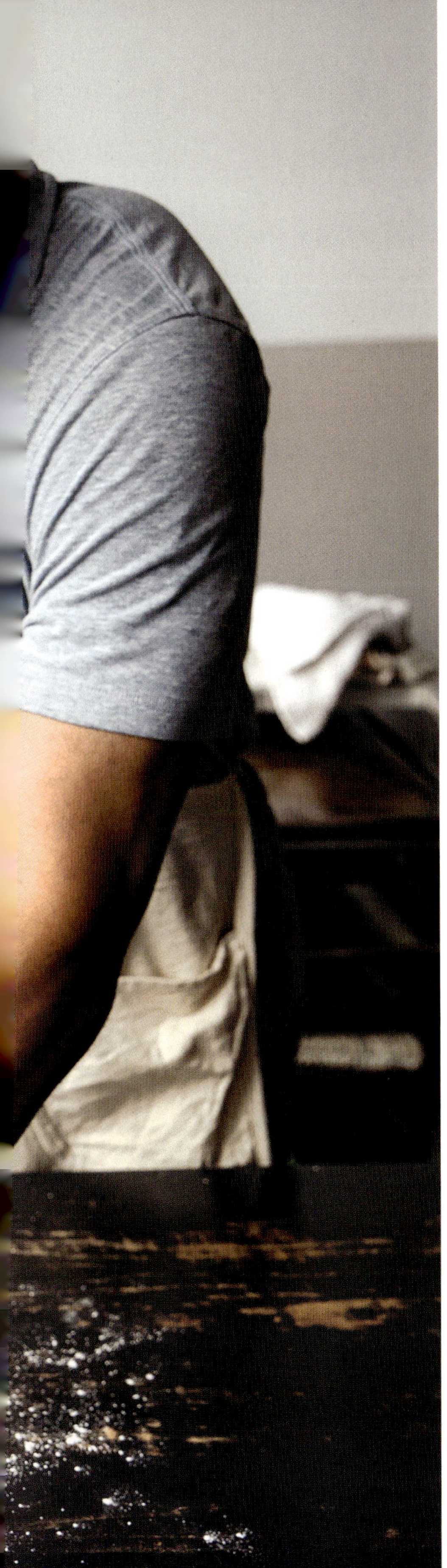

ON THE MENU

At a dinner party or any other communal meal gathering, the food is the centerpiece of the event, so it is important to choose a menu that is delicious and personal. You can find ideas in family recipes, cookbooks, recent travels, creative themes, and other culinary interests that you want to share with your guests.

Rather than a laborious hosting endeavor ahead of a busy week, this Sunday gathering needed to be as comforting for me to prepare for as it would be for my guests to attend. Whenever possible, I like to be in the kitchen with a family member or guest to enjoy the ritual of party preparation. For this dinner my husband, Jordan, was my sous-chef. For my menu, I drew inspiration from my time playing high school sports. We would often have team "pasta parties" a night or two before a big a game. The tradition was really about carb-loading, but it was also wonderful for bonding. When in doubt, a hearty pasta is a great anchor for a simple, satisfying menu.

Red Berry Salad (page 135)

Welcome Bread Board with Party Thyme Dip (page 99)

The Salad Is a Spectacle (page 102)

Dinner Party Pasta (page 104)

Peach Galette (page 106)

Vermouth Pitcher Spritzer (page 97)

Red wine

White wine

Water

Sparkling water

IN THE DETAILS

For me, Sunday has always been a day of worship, gathering, and respite from the outside world. As I imagined this dinner, I let my mind wander back to memories of my grandmother's house, where the décor was understated, the food felt like a warm hug, and time was always on our side. This was the feeling I wanted to share at my Sunday supper.

From Pantry to Party

To set this table, I turned to staples from my party pantry, including linen tablecloths and napkins and taper candles in soft neutral colors. I chose my white ceramic plates because I wanted the colors of the salad and the pasta to really stand out against the surrounding table elements. Alongside items from my pantry, I used fresh flowers and candlelight to bring just enough grandeur to an otherwise modestly arranged dinner table. I prefer to steam the linens, polish the glassware and cutlery, and set the table the night before because I do not like to be in a rush. I want to enjoy my rituals.

Setting the Table

Different dinner parties will require different place settings based on your menu and your desired level of formality. For this dinner, I used a more casual place setting technique to align with the menu and vibe of the occasion. Below is a guide for casual and formal dinner party settings. Both settings include a water glass, an all-purpose wineglass, a napkin, salad and entrée forks, salad and entrée knives, and a salad and entrée plate. The formal setting includes a Champagne flute, a bread plate and butter knife, place card, dessert spoon and dessert fork, and soupspoon. The formal setting also includes a more decorative napkin fold and a charger plate.

Casual

Formal

PRO TIPS

Creating Your Own Flower Arrangements

For this dinner's tablescape, I used white hydrangeas and small white carnations I found at the market the day before. When I am making my own floral arrangements, I like to choose either one type of flower in various colors or multiple flower varieties in the same color. Below are a few more best practices for sourcing and arranging your own flowers.

- **Purchase flowers one or two days before your event.** When purchasing flowers early, choose buds that have not yet opened up so they will be at their best on the day of your event. Refresh water daily to keep blooms thriving for as long as possible.
- **Inspect the stems before buying.** Look for green stems with a crisp cut and a white center. If stems appear yellow or brown, or have frayed edges, it is likely an indication that the blooms are not the freshest.
- **Select flowers based on their intended placement.** Ideally, flowers at the dinner table will not have a strong scent, so they do not compete with the food. Guest rooms and powder rooms, however, can always benefit from a fragrant flower selection.
- **Choose vessels with the dinner table in mind.** You want arrangements to be low, so guests can see the person sitting across from them. And if the dinner is family-style, you might want to consider slim vases and bud vases, so there is more real estate for shared plates.
- **Cut the stems at varying heights.** This brings depth and dimension to the arrangement. You should also cut stems on a sharp angle and remove any excess leaves, allowing the flower head to soak up as much water as possible.

Open Slow

For a Sunday dinner party, I like it to start in the early evening, around five p.m. This allows guests to ease into our time together and still make it home at an ideal hour to maintain their Sunday-night routines. Prior to dinner, guests can warm up their palates with light bites and sips, and break the ice with small talk. The French call this gathering time *l'apéro*, which is short for *apéritif*—an alcoholic beverage served before a meal to stimulate the appetite. It is typically served with appetizers or hors d'oeuvres, so I had a vermouth spritzer and a bread board ready to greet my guests. This filled the time while we waited for all the guests to arrive before sitting down at the table for dinner.

Vermouth Pitcher Spritzer

Serves 4 to 6

A traditional apéritif is a light, low-alcohol beverage that is dry, slightly bitter, or sparkling. The bitterness or acidity is what cleanses the palate and stimulates the appetite. I typically prefer a welcome apéritif that is slightly bitter and offers some floral notes. For that reason, I like to use Carpano Antica Formula vermouth. This recipe also works well with Lillet or Carpano Bianco, so do not be afraid to branch out and make substitutions with other fortified wines or liqueurs that complement your menu. Pre-batching this in a pitcher will get a beverage in front of guests on arrival. To maintain the effervescence of the mixture, prepare this drink just moments before guests arrive. I allow guests to choose their own garnish. My go-to is an orange slice, but other crowd-pleasers include a slice of grapefruit, an olive, or a sprig of rosemary.

1 (1-liter) bottle club soda, chilled

2 cups (480 ml) sweet vermouth, like Carpano Antica Formula vermouth

Ice cubes

Orange slices, grapefruit slices, pitted green olives, and/or rosemary sprigs, for garnish

Just before guests arrive, pour the club soda and vermouth into a pitcher. Stir to combine.

Fill each glass with ice cubes and pour in the spritzer. Allow guests to add their preferred garnish.

Welcome Bread Board

WITH PARTY THYME DIP

Serves 6

I love a bread board served with whipped butter and an herbaceous olive oil dip. I source my loaves from the local bakery. Typically, I gravitate toward a baguette, ciabatta, or focaccia. Choose breads that you like, and don't be afraid to include one that has a unique flavor. I offer two types of bread for a small group (six people or fewer), and three or four if I'm expecting a larger group. Depending on your guests' dietary restrictions, one of the options might need to be whole wheat or gluten-free.

PARTY THYME DIP

½ cup (120 ml) extra-virgin olive oil

1½ teaspoons fresh thyme leaves

1½ teaspoons thinly sliced fresh basil leaves

1½ teaspoons thinly sliced fresh oregano leaves

2 large garlic cloves, minced

½ teaspoon kosher salt

Freshly ground black pepper

ASSEMBLY

1 baguette

1 medium ciabatta or focaccia

1 (8-ounce/226 g) container whipped salted butter, at room temperature

Make the dip: In a small bowl, stir together the olive oil, thyme, basil, oregano, and garlic until well combined. Season with the salt and pepper to taste. Set aside at room temperature for about 15 minutes to allow the flavors to meld.

Assemble the board: Cut or tear the bread into 1-inch (2.5 cm) slices or pieces. Place the bread on a wooden serving board or plate. Place the whipped butter and olive oil dip in ramekins and serve immediately alongside the bread.

A House Playlist

I keep a "house playlist" of all my favorite songs to serve as lively background music for casual hosting. Your song curation should give guests an opportunity to learn more about you, your interests, recent travels, or feelings you want to share. The Hewett "house playlist" is filled with upbeat saxophone, piano, and horn across jazz, funk, and R & B genres. When my guests ask why, they learn that I played the saxophone in middle school. I was not very good at it (if my brother is in attendance, he will make sure that part of the story is clear), but my admiration for brass instruments started early and lives on through my house playlist, which includes:

- **"In a Sentimental Mood,"** Duke Ellington and John Coltrane
- **"Take Five,"** the Dave Brubeck Quartet
- **"So What,"** Miles Davis, featuring John Coltrane and Cannonball Adderley
- **"Barefoot Sunday Blues,"** the Cannonball Adderley Quartet
- **"Moanin',"** Art Blakey and the Jazz Messengers
- **"The Sun Died,"** Gene Ammons and Sonny Stitt
- **"Sweet Love,"** Najee
- **"I Feel It Coming,"** Nathan Allen
- **"Sunday Vibes,"** Masego & Medasin
- **"No Man No Cry,"** Jimmy Sax
- **"All Jazzed Up (and Nowhere to Go),"** Everette Harp
- **"Forbidden Fruit,"** Pamela Williams

The Salad Is a Spectacle

Serves 6

When all the guests have arrived, nothing brings them to the table faster than a bountiful dish ready to surprise and delight. Though simple, this salad grabs guests' attention with fresh, colorful vegetables, and edible flowers for garnish.

VINAIGRETTE

½ small shallot, finely chopped

2 garlic cloves, minced

2 tablespoons red wine vinegar

2 tablespoons fresh orange juice

1 teaspoon Dijon mustard

1 teaspoon honey

¼ teaspoon kosher salt, plus more if needed

⅛ teaspoon freshly ground black pepper, plus more if needed

¼ cup (60 ml) extra-virgin olive oil

SALAD

4 medium heads Little Gem lettuce, coarsely chopped

2 tablespoons extra-virgin olive oil

Kosher salt and freshly ground black pepper

3 medium rainbow carrots

2 breakfast radishes, thinly sliced

2 watermelon radishes, thinly sliced

1 small red onion, thinly sliced

6 ounces (170 g) feta cheese, drained and crumbled

2 tablespoons finely chopped fresh parsley

2 tablespoons chopped fresh dill

Microgreens, for garnish

Edible flowers, such as pansies, lavender, micro orchids, daisies, cucumber flowers, or squash blossoms, for garnish

Make the vinaigrette: In a small bowl, whisk together the shallot, garlic, vinegar, orange juice, mustard, honey, salt, and pepper until well combined. Slowly whisk in the olive oil until well combined and emulsified. Taste and season with additional salt and pepper, if desired. Set aside.

Make the salad: Place the lettuce in a large serving bowl. Drizzle the olive oil over the lettuce and season with salt and pepper to taste; toss gently to coat. Drizzle one-quarter of the vinaigrette over the lettuce; toss again to coat. Set aside.

Fill a large bowl with ice and cold water. Use a vegetable peeler to shave the carrots from stem to tip, forming curls. Submerge the strips in the ice bath for about 2 minutes to set the curls. Drain well and pat dry with paper towels.

Transfer the carrot curls to a medium bowl. Add the breakfast radishes, watermelon radishes, onion, and one-third of the remaining vinaigrette; gently toss to combine. Taste and season with salt and pepper.

Add the vegetable mixture to the bowl of lettuce. Sprinkle with the feta, parsley, and dill. Garnish with microgreens and edible flowers. Serve immediately, with the remaining vinaigrette on the side.

Dinner Party Pasta

Serves 6 to 8

At my high school sports teams' pasta parties, I had Italian spaghetti, Haitian spaghetti, Dominican spaghetti, Southern baked spaghetti, and Indian spaghetti. Every family (including mine) had its own twist, and every version was as good as the one before. When I make spaghetti, I like to serve it with a hearty meat sauce that is brightened by a bit of white wine and packs a little spice from the cubanelle pepper.

2 tablespoons extra-virgin olive oil

1 small onion, finely chopped

1 large carrot, finely chopped

1 large celery stalk, finely chopped

6 garlic cloves, minced

1 small cubanelle pepper, seeded and finely chopped

1½ teaspoons kosher salt, plus more as needed

¾ teaspoon freshly ground black pepper, plus more as needed

1 pound (455 g) 80% lean ground beef, preferably grass-fed

8 ounces (225 g) sweet Italian sausage, casings removed

1 cup (240 ml) dry white wine (such as pinot grigio, sauvignon blanc, or chardonnay)

1 (28-ounce/794 g) can whole peeled tomatoes, with their juices

1 (6-ounce/170 g) can tomato paste

In a large Dutch oven, heat the olive oil over medium heat. Add the onion and cook, stirring occasionally, until translucent, about 5 minutes. Add the carrot and celery and cook, stirring occasionally, until the vegetables are tender, 3 to 4 minutes. Stir in the garlic and cubanelle. Cook until the garlic is fragrant but not browned, about 1 minute. Season with the salt and black pepper.

Add the ground beef and sausage and cook, stirring occasionally and breaking up the meat as it cooks, until browned, 10 to 12 minutes. Add the wine and simmer until it has mostly evaporated, about 4 minutes. Add the tomatoes (with their juices) and tomato paste and stir until well combined.

Add the stock, basil, oregano, thyme, red pepper flakes, and bay leaves. Reduce the heat to low to maintain a slow simmer. Cook, uncovered, stirring occasionally, until the liquid has almost completely reduced and the sauce is thick, about 3 hours. If the sauce looks dry or the liquid is evaporating too quickly, add more stock ½ cup (120 ml) at a time.

Meanwhile, cook the pasta according to the package instructions. Reserve 1½ cups (360 ml) of the pasta cooking water, then drain the pasta.

- 1 cup (240 ml) beef stock, plus more as needed
- 1 tablespoon chopped fresh basil leaves
- 1 tablespoon dried oregano
- 1 tablespoon fresh thyme leaves
- 1 tablespoon red pepper flakes, plus more for serving
- 2 bay leaves
- 1 pound (455 g) dried spaghetti
- Grated Parmesan cheese, for serving

Transfer the pasta to a large pan or serving bowl, add the sauce, and toss, adding the reserved pasta water ¼ cup (60 ml) at a time until the pasta is evenly coated with the sauce. Season with salt and black pepper.

Serve immediately, with Parmesan and additional red pepper flakes on the side.

Peach Galette

Serves 8

As soon as peaches are in season, I'm first in line at the market, and I turn to a galette whenever I don't want to break out a pie dish or make a cobbler. I find a galette very forgiving. You don't have to worry about the dough being perfectly rolled, folded, or pinched. If peaches are not in season, you can reach for other fruits, like apples, strawberries, cherries, or blackberries.

DOUGH

2½ cups (315 g) unbleached all-purpose flour, plus more for dusting

1 tablespoon granulated sugar

1 teaspoon baking powder

1 teaspoon fine sea salt

1 cup (2 sticks/227 g) unsalted butter, cubed and chilled

½ cup (120 ml) ice water

PEACH FILLING

6 large ripe peaches, peeled, pitted, and thinly sliced into half-moons

⅓ cup firmly packed (150 g) dark brown sugar

2 tablespoons cornstarch

1 teaspoon fresh lemon juice

½ teaspoon ground cinnamon

½ teaspoon ground nutmeg

1 large egg

1 tablespoon water

2 tablespoons turbinado sugar

Leaves from 2 thyme sprigs (optional)

Make the dough: In a medium bowl or a food processor, combine the flour, granulated sugar, baking powder, and salt. Add the cold butter cubes and toss or pulse until they are coated in the flour mixture, then use a pastry blender or pulse until the butter is combined and the mixture is crumbly in texture. Slowly drizzle in half the ice water, blending or pulsing as the dough begins to come together. As the dough gets smoother, add the remaining ice water 1 tablespoon at a time until a dough ball forms (you may not need all the water).

Transfer the dough to an unfloured work surface. Begin kneading with the palm of one hand, pushing the dough down and away from you and then gathering it back. Repeat this process two or three times, then form the dough into a flat 1-inch-thick (2.5 cm) disk. Wrap in plastic wrap and refrigerate for at least 1 hour or up to overnight.

Meanwhile, make the filling: Place the peaches in a medium bowl and add the brown sugar, cornstarch, lemon juice, cinnamon, and nutmeg. Gently fold until the peaches are evenly coated.

Preheat the oven to 400°F (200°C). Line a large baking sheet with parchment paper.

Remove the dough from the refrigerator. If it was chilled overnight, let it sit at room temperature for 10 minutes before rolling. Unwrap the dough and place it on a lightly floured surface, then lightly flour the dough. Roll the dough into a large round, about 14 inches (36 cm) in diameter. Transfer the dough to the prepared baking sheet.

In a small bowl, whisk the egg and water until well combined to make an egg wash.

Arrange the peaches in a circle starting from the center of the dough and ending 2 to 3 inches (5 to 7 cm) from the edge. Brush some of the egg wash over the exposed portion of the dough, then fold the dough toward the center, overlapping the edge and pinching it together every 2 inches (5 cm) to create loose pleats. Brush more of the egg wash over the dough and sprinkle with the turbinado sugar.

Bake for about 25 minutes, until the crust is golden brown and the fruit is bubbling. Serve warm or at room temperature. Finish with thyme leaves, if desired. The galette can be stored, covered, at room temperature for up to 1 day.

Let Them Linger

After dessert, when bellies are full and bottles are empty, resist the urge to get up and start cleaning. If guests look comfortable, let them stay at the table and talk for a while. During this time, I like to bring out coffee and tea, as well as mints. You might also bring out a digestif or dessert wine. I've come to know this after-dinner linger as the time when real bonds form. In fact, in Latin American countries they even have a special name for this tradition of relaxing at the table after dinner—it's called *sobremesa*, and it is a ritual not to be skipped. Let the dishes pile up high and the candles burn down low so you can be a present host as the conversation flows past dinner and the night finds its natural end.

THE SEND-OFF

Because I host dinner parties often, I created a supper club punch card to share with my family and friends. Each time they attend, they get a stamp. It is a fun way to keep track of the dinner experiences we've had together, and it helps keep us accountable for gathering as often as we can. If you enjoy cooking or hosting dinner parties, create your own supper club card. When a card is full, you can delight your guests with a fun surprise. This can be a special dessert, the opportunity to propose the next dinner theme, or a party favor or small gift (see page 218 for inspiration).

SEASON:
Spring

GUEST COUNT:
8

PLANNING TIME:
3 weeks

Crafts & Crudités

FOR A CREATIVE REPRIEVE

Hobbies can bring energy and zest to our lives. And having a community to engage in hobbies with makes the experience even more fulfilling. Crafting has always fueled how I live and work. There are so many elements of our day-to-day lives that can seem monotonous and unvarying, making it easy to feel stuck in a rut. When I feel anxious or uninspired, I turn to crafts for moments of respite. Hosting artsy afternoons with friends allows me to share this restorative time with others.

Craft parties have become a fresh source of inspiration for my most creative friends. When I started these monthly gatherings, the guests were all friends of mine, but they were not yet all friends with each other. In developing the guest list, I prioritized a shared interest in crafting and desire for a creative outlet because this common ground would become the foundation for my friends to build their own relationships on as the parties continued.

When it comes to craft parties, I think you get bonus points when you choose a craft that is wearable or edible. At this gathering of my monthly craft crew, the craft was cake decorating.

ON THE MENU

I hosted this event in the late afternoon, so I knew I could keep the menu to light refreshments. I assembled a crudités platter using a bounty of fresh vegetable from the farmers' market to offer guests a few healthy nibbles before their inevitable date with a slice of cake.

Crudités platter (see page 118)

Rosé

Iced tea

Cucumber-infused water

IN THE DETAILS

As I planned this party, my focus was on keeping all the elements light and sweet (a sentiment that would later inspire the craft itself). The feeling I wanted to capture was that of a leisurely Saturday morning when you can wake up slow, put on your favorite playlist, and open all the windows to let the fresh spring air flow through your space.

Keep It Light & Whimsical

I wanted bright colors and quaint details to take the lead here, to invoke a playful energy that would help my guests relax and get creative. It is particularly important to me that the décor at a craft party isn't too fancy because it makes people feel stiff or like what they create has to be perfect in order to belong. Keep the décor simple and provide enough space for guests to spread out, get a little messy, and figure it out as they go.

Planning Was a Piece of Cake

I contacted one of my favorite bakers, Jenneh Kaikai from Pelah Kitchen in Brooklyn, and asked her to prepare eight 6-inch (15 cm) cakes; I opted for pistachio, espresso chocolate, and lemon butter. I knew that my group did not have any dietary restrictions, so each cake was frosted with the same Swiss meringue buttercream and the cakes were distributed at random, adding a layer of surprise and delight to the experience. (If your group has dietary restrictions or notable preferences when it comes to dessert, be sure to request cake flavors and frostings accordingly.)

Options Should Be Plentiful

For a cake-decorating party, the creative energy comes from the different flavors, colors, textures, and sizes of the toppings. You can find options at your local market or party supply store, as well as on Etsy. My options included buttercream frosting in various colors, fresh berries, dehydrated citrus slices, edible flower petals, edible glitter, maraschino cherries, and sprinkles. The more toppings, the more creatively expressive your guests can be. This fondness for variety can carry over to other crafts, too. If you're drawing, you may want pencils in different colors; if you're making collages, consider the paper, and if you are making jewelry, get extra charms.

An Artful Serving of Veggies

Once arrangements for the main attraction were in place, I turned my attention to the other party elements. The focus of this party was the craft, and the timing was right between brunch and dinner, so there was little pressure to offer a full meal. I opted for serving a crudités platter with a few of my favorite dips; it is a great way to present the bounty of a season. I picked up vegetables and dips at the farmers' market that morning. Below are a few tips for assembling your own grazing boards.

1. Choose a colorful assortment of the best-quality, in-season vegetables. In general, I offer six types (estimating 4 to 6 ounces/ 120 to 160 g per person). I chose cauliflower, purple cauliflower, snap peas, radishes, asparagus, tricolor carrots, and cucumbers.
2. You can make dips from scratch or pick up options from your local purveyor. Estimate about ¼ cup (85 grams) of dip(s), total, per person. My crudités platter included hummus, tzatziki, and beet dip.
3. Wash your vegetables and prepare your dips before guests arrive. Portion your offering to serve about half of the veggies and dips to start and replenish when needed.
4. When it comes to getting the veggies to the table, depending on your party size, you might want to have a single platter, arrange a full table spread buffet-style, or make individual paper boats that guests can grab and go.
5. Dress up your board with fresh herbs and edible flowers, if desired.

Add Dazzle to the Details

At the refreshment table, the signature beverage was an iced sweet tea labeled "Creativi-tea" with drink tags. I like adding drink tags, functionally so everyone can keep track of their glass, but also to add a little extra effort to an otherwise simple offering. You can find talented makers on Etsy for these drink tags, as well as for other customizable details like stir sticks, glassware stem charms, edible cocktail toppers, and beverage napkins.

A Saturday Morning Playlist

For this playlist, I pulled inspiration from my weekend-morning cleaning playlist. I wanted easy-listening music that my guests would also recognize and sing along to while decorating their cakes.

- **"My Boo,"** Usher and Alicia Keys
- **"Doo Wop (That Thing),"** Lauryn Hill
- **"Say My Name,"** Destiny's Child
- **"Golden,"** Jill Scott
- **"Get Me Bodied,"** Beyoncé
- **"Fantasy,"** Mariah Carey
- **"Baby It's You,"** JoJo
- **"All Around the World,"** Lisa Stansfield
- **"U Remind Me,"** Usher
- **"This Love,"** Maroon 5
- **"Rock the Boat,"** Aaliyah
- **"Into You,"** Fabolous, featuring Tamia

Make It a Club

As you explore what craft and cadence is best for your group, you should also discuss how you will approach the crafts. You might find that you have particularly curious friends who are open to trying a different craft each month. Below, you can find some crafty ideas to consider. Alternatively, you might have a group that really enjoys painting; then, *what* you paint or with what type of paint (e.g., watercolor or acrylic) is where you will find your creative variation. When everyone is enthusiastic about the craft particulars, it will make it easier for everyone to prioritize this leisurely time together.

- Air-dry-clay sculpting
- Card making
- Collage making or scrapbooking
- Cookie decorating
- Coloring or painting
- Customizing clothing, accessories, or home goods
- Drawing or doodling
- Flower arranging or flower crown making
- Jewelry making
- Knitting or crocheting
- Paper flower making
- Pottery or vase decorating
- Wreath making

THE SEND-OFF

After all their hard work, you want to ensure that guests can take their creations home with them. For this gathering, I used craft paper boxes with a clear window lid so that each cake's design could still be admired through the box. Based on your chosen craft, make sure you have the right take-home containers for easy transport.

SEASON:
Summer

GUEST COUNT:
30+

PLANNING TIME:
4 weeks

The Cookout

FOR COMMUNITY HEALING

To me, cookouts have become synonymous with freedom. Not only because of the holidays that are typically anchored to a cookout, but for the energy that surrounds these events. These parties are often defined by lively music, a hot grill, and a cooler full of cold drinks. But these are just the surface elements. At its core, the cookout is a way for your entire village to experience leisure and joy.

I have the fondest memories of my family's cookouts, after-church gatherings, and college homecoming weekends. When I am hosting the cookout, I invite family, friends, and neighbors alike. I protect the spirit of the gathering by keeping an open-door policy for kids and plus-multiples. I find it is particularly important to make these gatherings a full village affair because this time gathering across generations creates a sense of belonging that we need at every age and stage of life.

For this event, we were celebrating Juneteenth—a holiday marking the end of slavery and a celebration of freedom for all people in the United States. This occasion was an opportunity to honor tradition and keep history alive. My hope in hosting was for the fellowship of this day to also serve as a reminder that we have a future and freedoms worth fighting for.

ON THE MENU

Grilled meats and vegetables were the centerpieces of my cookout menu. When I am entertaining outside on a hot day, I like to serve grilled dishes with cold sides and desserts, and plenty of cold beverages. In my experience, a cookout is an hours-long affair. I start the party around 1 or 2 p.m., and I expect it to go well past sunset. Because of this, the menu is lengthy, and I think of it in courses (even if that is not formally stated). I begin with fruit salad, burgers, and hot dogs, and as the event moves into the late afternoon and evening, I bring out ribs, chicken, skewers, grilled corn, and sides.

Red Berry Salad (page 135)
Beef and veggie burgers
Hot dogs
Sausage links
Ribs
Grilled chicken
Grilled corn
Grilled vegetable skewers
Garden salad
Potato salad
Ice pops
Ice cream and sorbet

Red Drink (page 133)
Beer
Sangria
Sodas and juices
Juices
Water

IN THE DETAILS

The cookout is a sacred space for family, friends, and neighbors, and making this space feel vibrant and victorious is always my primary goal. I accomplish this with an abundance of food, intentional color choices, and music that keeps my guests moving and grooving. I dressed up picnic tables with tablecloths, place mats, fruits, and flowers from the garden (I like layering different materials, colors, and patterns whenever I am entertaining alfresco).

Entertaining Across Generations

Hosting a large group across generations can be challenging because you have to make accommodations for individuals of all ages when it comes to food, drinks, seating, music, and entertainment. As you review your guest list, grab your entertaining journal and write down the names of the youngest guest and the eldest. Underneath each name, make a short list of needs. For small children, that might include a particular food and poolside safety measures. For extra-grown folks, you might want to have more seat cushions.

Be a Little Shady

In the days leading up to my event, I examine my outdoor space at different times throughout the day and take note of where guests can find shade. I tailor my setup according to the shade, and if its limited, I make a plan for how I can create more with umbrellas or tents.

PRO TIPS

Grilling

If you fire up the grill, they will come. This is what I learned watching my dad grill for our family cookouts. He had his own routine, too: He would make himself an iced tea, set up his station, turn on his music, and soon enough, burgers, hot dogs, ribs, and sausages would find their way to our plates. When it was my turn to get on the grill, I was intimidated at first. Eventually, I found my own routine. Here are a few tips that helped me build my confidence.

- **Use the right tools for the task.** Make sure you've collected the appropriate grill-specific tools, including tongs, a cleaning brush, heavy-duty gloves, a meat thermometer, and any other desired grill accessories (e.g., a basting brush, water-soaked skewers, or a grill basket).
- **Do your mise en place.** You don't want to leave the grill unattended, so be sure to gather all your ingredients and supplies before you even turn it on. This includes the tools mentioned above, as well as sauces or seasonings, large trays or baking sheets, foil, a kitchen towel, and a fire extinguisher.
- **Use temperature to improve your technique.** Bringing your meats to room temperature before grilling is an easy way to cook the meat more evenly and get that picturesque sear.
- **Clean as you go.** Use a grill brush to clean your grill grates before and after each use to eliminate food and grease buildup. Before grilling, you can deglaze your grill with onion to remove any lingering material from the grates and add a very mild flavor to the grates: First, preheat your grill, and once the grates are hot, use a grill brush to remove any buildup. Then, peel and halve an onion and rub it down the hot grates of the grill. This cleaning can help prevent flame flare-ups. If you're grilling steaks or chicken, trimming the excess fat will also help.
- **Explore flavorful hacks.** If you don't have a cedar plank, you can use sliced lemon wheels to create a nonstick surface for fish—or even chicken. Foil can be used to create a sealed pouch for shellfish and vegetables.

Serve Something Chill

With so much hot food coming off the grill, I like to have plenty of chilled beverages and sides to help guests beat the heat. I recommend keeping a cooler overflowing with beverages, a punch bowl on ice, and a medley of salads (fruit salad, potato salad, and a fresh garden salad will offer your guests some nice variety).

Red Drink

Serves 15

To me, it's not a party if there isn't a punch bowl filled with a drink that's just a little sweet and most certainly spiked. On Juneteenth, it is tradition to serve red foods and beverages because red is a symbol of the profound sacrifice and resilience of African American people. This punch gets its red hue from a homemade sorrel syrup, which can be made in advance and stored in an airtight container for up to a week.

SORREL SYRUP

4 cups (1 L) water

1½ cups (300 g) sugar

1 cup (1½ ounces/40 g) organic cut and sifted dried hibiscus flowers

2 cinnamon sticks

PUNCH

2 (2 L) bottles club soda

1 cup (240 ml) dark rum

Juice of 2 large lemons

Ice cubes

4 lemons, sliced into wheels and seeded, for garnish

Make the syrup: In a medium pot, combine the water and sugar and bring to a boil over medium-high heat, stirring until the sugar has dissolved.

Add the hibiscus flowers and cinnamon sticks, and stir until the flowers start to soften. Reduce the heat to medium to maintain a gentle boil. Cook, stirring occasionally, until the syrup is deep red in color and infused with a floral flavor, about 20 minutes. Remove from the heat and let stand for 5 minutes.

Strain the mixture through a fine-mesh sieve into a bowl, pressing on the solids to extract all the liquid; discard the solids. Let the syrup cool completely before using or storing, about 30 minutes. (The sorrel syrup can be stored in an airtight container in the refrigerator for up to a week.)

Make the punch: In a large punch bowl, stir together the club soda, 1 cup (240 ml) of the sorrel syrup, the rum, and the lemon juice to combine. Serve with ice and garnish with lemon wheels.

Red Berry Salad

Serves 12

This salad combines my favorite summer fruits and is my go-to for outdoor entertaining. I like to serve it as a welcome dish when guests are arriving, but it also works alongside desserts. It is best to wash and dry all the fruits and store them in separate airtight containers in the refrigerator, combining them and adding the lime juice, zest, and mint just before serving.

2 cups (250 g) raspberries

2 cups (330 g) sliced strawberries

2 cups (300 g) cherries, pitted and halved

Zest and juice of 1 lime

Fresh mint leaves, for garnish

Place the raspberries, strawberries, cherries, lime zest, and lime juice in a large bowl. Gently stir with a rubber spatula until combined. Transfer to a serving dish and garnish with mint. Refrigerate until chilled, then serve cold.

A Good Times Playlist

For a cookout, I like to have music that spans generations and genres—including R & B, disco, and hip-hop. I want the music to inspire guests to sing along at the start and get up and dance as the night goes on. Below are songs I shared with the DJ to guide the music selections for this event. See page 215 for tips on hiring a DJ; and if you're making your own playlist, ensure that it's a long one, as the party often carries on for hours.

- **"Family Affair,"** Mary J. Blige
- **"Fantastic Voyage,"** Lakeside
- **"Square Biz,"** Teena Marie
- **"Fool's Paradise,"** Meli'sa Morgan
- **"Let's Groove,"** Earth, Wind & Fire
- **"Never Too Much,"** Luther Vandross
- **"Before I Let Go,"** Maze, featuring Frankie Beverly
- **"Hey Mr. D.J.,"** Zhané
- **"Essence,"** Wizkid, featuring Tems
- **"Return of the Mack,"** Mark Morrison
- **"Honey,"** Mariah Carey
- **"Can't Get Enough,"** Tamia

Ideas for Outdoor Games

When I was growing up, our family cookouts had grandpas playing backgammon in the shade, grown folks playing spades, a basketball hoop and two jump ropes for double Dutch for the older cousins, and a ring toss game for the littlest ones. Here are a few games that are great for cookouts and entertaining alfresco. (Remember: Having something captivating for the kids will ensure that the adults can enjoy their time, too.)

FOR ADULTS

Backgammon
Bocce ball
Cards
Connect Four
Cornhole
Croquet
Dominoes
Jenga

FOR KIDS

Basketball
Bubbles or a bubble maker
Double Dutch
Freeze dancing
Hopscotch
Musical chairs
Relay races
Ring toss
Twister
Water balloon games

THE SEND-OFF

For dessert at a summertime event, opt for something cool. You can turn to ice pops, ice cream, semifreddos, or all of the above. Remember, how you present these desserts is an opportunity for spectacle. For this gathering, I used a Champagne bucket to serve an assortment of freeze pops.

UNO

SEASON:
Fall

GUEST COUNT:
6

PLANNING TIME:
3 weeks

Playtime & Provisions

FOR GAME NIGHT WITH YOUR FAVES

When I want to feel the spirit of togetherness among friends, family members, neighbors, or colleagues, I host a game night. There is a natural conviviality that surrounds such an event. It's jovial and lighthearted in nature, but every circle has that one game that brings out the healthy competition that is energizing for everyone involved. In college, my roommates and I would host Taboo nights for our friends. Our living room would echo with laughter and spirited debate well into the early morning. And since getting together with my husband, I've learned that if you can walk away victorious from a round of Settlers of Catan with the Hewetts, you'll earn their respect.

For this get-together, I decided we would play UNO! It's a simple game, yet it's stimulating and strategic and allows the group to chat, listen to music, and enjoy light refreshments while playing. Whatever game you choose, these events can be a gateway to stronger relationships, an opportunity to cast worries aside and focus on some good clean fun.

ON THE MENU

I hosted this event in the late evening, so the menu was composed of light refreshments for guests to snack on during the games, as well as classic cocktails rechristened with fun game-related names.

Charcuterie for Champions (see page 148)

Popcorn

Peanut M&M's

Sour gummy bears

Martini

Old-Fashioned

Beer

Wine

Water

IN THE DETAILS

With UNO! on the table, I opted for dim lighting, a dark round table, and textured glassware. These elements ensured that it would feel like an adult game night even if the game on the table was a childhood favorite.

But First, the Rules

It is important to start the night with an overview of the game's rules. This is critical even when playing a familiar game like UNO! At my game night, you can stack a +2 and a +4, even if the official rules of UNO! do not agree. After you've covered the rules, give your guests a general sense of how the night will flow (i.e., the number of game rounds, whether it will be played tournament style or using a point system, etc.). You can also take this time to set intentions and make a fun toast before the games begin.

PRO TIPS

Organizing a Game Night

- **Game on!** As you consider what game (or games) to play, consider your favorites, and don't be afraid to ask a few of your guests to weigh in. Your choice of game can influence the ideal party size, guest list, and creative details. Some options to consider: bingo, Codenames, American mahjong, poker, Settlers of Catan, spades, trivia games, or charades.
- **Prioritize familiarity among guests.** While I am known to mix it up for other hosting occasions, on game night, I like to invite a close-knit friend group or other couples. I find that this level of acquaintance brings out the competitive spirit you need for game night.
- **Keep a close eye on your RSVPs.** While the party is a casual one, you want to make sure you end up with the right number of participants for the game. If guests will be competing in pairs, make sure everyone knows that game night is BYOP (bring your own partner). If you will be assigning teams, make sure you have a balance of personalities that like to lead and agreeable team players.
- **Choose your format wisely.** You'll want to organize your event in a way that is most fitting for the game, the size of your entertaining space, the number of guests, and the interests of your group. The simplest approach is a single game that involves all the guests competing individually or in teams. You may also arrange the competition as a tournament, with a game that involves small groups or pairs. (Depending on the party size and the length of the game, you can have multiple games running simultaneously or have one game going at a time while other guests watch and wait for their turn.)
- **Go screen-free.** Capture guests' undivided attention by creating a phone pile at the game table. This offers a refreshing opportunity for guests to enjoy the evening without distractions from the outside world. The first person to reach for their phone during gameplay loses a point for their team.

A Fanciful Concession Stand

My game-night welcome table is a classy concession stand with snacks and sips for guests to enjoy throughout the night. The station included peanut M&M's, sour gummy bears, and popcorn. (I season my popcorn with a generous dash of chipotle chili powder, a pinch of garlic powder, lime zest, and salt.) For beverages, I renamed cocktails to match our theme, offering a "You Play a Dirty Game Martini" and an "Old-Fashioned Rule Follower" (served with dice-shaped ice for added amusement).

Charcuterie for Champions

I hosted this get-together in the late evening, so there was no expectation for a full dinner. When this is the case, I like to prepare a charcuterie board with delicious cheeses, cured meats, and an abundance of accompaniments to explore. I offered this board on arrival so guests could fill their little plates before sitting down for games. (I opted to arrange this spread on a serving platter with handles so I could easily come around the table to offer replenishments.)

CHEESE

As a starting point, I like to offer at least one soft cheese, one semi-firm cheese, and one hard cheese (my favorites are listed below). As you explore different cheeses, consider variation in type of milk (e.g., cow's, sheep's, or goat's) or country of origin. You can estimate about 2 ounces (55 g) of cheese per person. Take the cheese out of the refrigerator one hour before serving.

- Soft cheeses: Brie, Bûcheron, Camembert, chèvre, ricotta
- Semi-firm cheeses: Cheddar, Comté, Gruyère, Manchego
- Hard cheeses: Gouda, Parmigiano-Reggiano, Pecorino Romano

BREADS & CRACKERS

Select two or three cracker and bread options. For breads, pre-slice or tear them to make the board more approachable for guests. Depending on your guests' dietary restrictions or allergies, you might offer a gluten-free bread or vegan crackers as well. My go-to crowd pleasers include:

- Baguette
- Croccantinis or artisanal crunchy, salty crackers
- Multigrain crackers
- Sourdough

ACCOMPANIMENTS

Offer six to eight accompaniments, with a good balance of savory and sweet options (my favorites are below). Serve these accompaniments in small bowls and ramekins and replenish as needed.

- Cured meats (chorizo, jambon de Bayonne, jamon Ibérico, pepperoni, prosciutto, soppressata)
- Dried fruits such as mangoes and apricots
- Fresh fruits (figs, berries, grapes, pomegranate seeds, olives, tomatoes)
- Honey or honeycombs
- Jams such as apricot and berry
- Nuts such as almonds, cashews, and walnuts

A Players' Club Playlist

With a night of fierce competition ahead, I wanted the music to have a playful and mid-tempo sound that would be catchy and recognizable for my guests.

- **"This Is How We Do It,"** Montell Jordan, featuring Wino
- **"Players Gon' Play,"** 3LW
- **"Waterfalls,"** TLC
- **"Fabulous,"** Jaheim, featuring Tha Rayne
- **"U Remind Me,"** Usher
- **"All for You,"** Janet Jackson
- **"Can We Talk,"** Tevin Campbell
- **"Where the Party At,"** Jagged Edge, featuring Nelly
- **"Frontin',"** Pharrell Williams, featuring Jay-Z
- **"Squabble Up,"** Kendrick Lamar
- **"Paradise,"** LL Cool J
- **"Love Me JeJe,"** Tems

End on a High Note

Close out the evening with a final parting toast to bring the group back to a collective mindset. Thank everyone for coming, congratulate the winner(s), and reinforce the message that time for play will keep us together.

THE SEND-OFF

Awarding a trophy is a fun way to end game night. I found my mini vintage trophy at my local thrift store and I thought it would bring a lighthearted touch to nights of spirited competition. I often present this trophy along with chocolate treats to share with other players. The winner can bring the mini trophy home, but they must return for the next game night ready to compete again.

SEASON:
Fall

GUEST COUNT:
12

PLANNING TIME:
5 weeks

Friendsgiving Potluck

FOR SHARING YOUR HOSTING RESPONSIBILITIES

Oftentimes, we regard hosting as a solo endeavor, but I encourage you to embrace a more community-oriented approach and make your next dinner party a potluck. It makes the meal experience a communal effort, with each guest bringing a dish to share with the group. This party format becomes especially useful during the holiday season or when hosting larger gatherings.

I love learning about food and family traditions through the dishes guests bring to a potluck. At these events, we nourish our bodies and also feed our curious minds. For this occasion, I wanted to spend time with the chefs, beverage professionals, event planners, and florists I work with for To Be Hosted events. For work, we all make plans for others, so the intention for this dinner was to spend time taking care of each other. I knew that all our unique perspectives on hospitality would lead to rich table conversations and thoughtful potluck contributions.

The potluck-style format was the perfect way to celebrate each of my guests' talents. With a florist and a sommelier on the guest list, we had an extra-beautiful table setting and the perfect wine pairings. When guests RSVP'd, I asked what they planned to contribute to ensure that all our needs were covered. I also collected playlist suggestions, so every detail was a collective effort.

ON THE MENU

For a potluck, the menu contributions typically reflect a personal favorite or a coveted family recipe, making the gathering rich with personal stories and diverse flavors. When preparing for a big feast, I like to have plenty of wine to complement the meal.

For wines, dinner party guest and sommelier Wendell "DJ" Alston selected bottles that would pair well with our menu. When shopping for wine, DJ recommends being descriptive when telling the wine seller about the flavors and textures of the foods on the menu to get the best recommendations. "When I am making selections, I like the wine and food to hit your taste buds in the same way," DJ shared. "I pair acidic foods with white wines that have citrus notes. I pair hearty red meats with full-bodied red wines. For this potluck, I brought a crisp Sancerre to pair with the fresh acidity of Aretah's salsa verde and a California zinfandel that could stand up to the heartiness of Mike's chili."

Roasted chicken with Aretah Ettarh's
Pumpkin Seed Salsa Verde (page 163)

Jahvel Fraser's Roasted Veggie Salad (page 164)

Mike Carter's Smoked Short Rib Chili (page 166)

Camari Mick's Apple Tarte Tatin (page 168)

Auzerais Bellamy's German Chocolate Blondies (page 170)

Red wine

White wine

Water

Sparkling water

A Playlist by Friends

To bring some potluck energy to the playlist, too, I asked guests to include a song request with their RSVP. This way, the playlist was composed of music that guests would love.

- **"BMF,"** SZA (from chef Aretah Ettarh)
- **"Bodyguard,"** Beyoncé (from event planner Alia Hodge)
- **"Sky Walker,"** Miguel, featuring Travis Scott (from chef Jahvel Fraser)
- **"Sprinkle Me,"** Premo Rice (from chef Mike Carter)
- **"Lose Yourself to Dance,"** Daft Punk, featuring Pharrell Williams (from florist Emily Scott)
- **"I Like It,"** DeBarge (my selection)
- **"Don't Ask My Neighbors,"** the Emotions (from pastry chef Auzerais Bellamy)
- **"A House Is Not a Home,"** Luther Vandross (from pastry chef Camari Mick)
- **"Green Papaya,"** Lianne La Havas (from photographer Rashida Zagon)
- **"Lullaby,"** JayDon and Paradise (from photographer Wendell "DJ" Alston)
- **"Traitor Joe,"** Mia Taylor (from musician Mia Taylor)
- **"Impatient,"** Josh Dean (from musician Josh Dean)

IN THE DETAILS

The holiday season is one of my favorite times to host and gather with family and chosen family. In putting this event together, I wanted to focus on the details that would make my guests feel the magic of the holiday season. I know that sounds cliché, but with a full house, a well adorned table, and thoughtful details, the enchantment is sure to follow.

An Unexpected Collection

The spirit of a potluck is to honor what everyone brings to the table and illustrate how beautifully these things can go together. I approached the tablescape in the same way, making use of what I already had in my party pantry. I chose a combination of gold, silver, and clear acrylic candleholders with taper candles in a variety of textures (including fluted, spiraled, and honeycombed). Dinner party guest and florist Emily Scott of Floriconvento recommended dried hydrangeas, spent rosebushes, and yellowing foliage like ginkgo leaves and dried wild grasses, which I paired with brighter colors—red, orange, and purple. Alongside the flowers and candles, I placed small bowls with fruits, nuts, and seeds. The edible items added visual interest and gave guests something to nibble on before dinner.

PRO TIPS

Seating Arrangements

When hosting a communal meal for six or more guests, I recommend assigning seats. While this might seem like a practice reserved for formal occasions, at casual gatherings it reinforces the message that everyone has a place at your table. And for larger gatherings, assigned seats will eliminate any awkward game of musical chairs (unless it is game night—in which case musical chairs sounds fun). Here are a few tips for approaching your seating chart, and you can find place card inspiration on page 217.

- **Sketch it out.** When I am working on my seating charts, I start by drawing the table and seats on a page in my entertaining journal. Then I write everyone's name down on small sticky notes, so I can adjust their seats more easily as I work toward the final arrangement.
- **Find the right combinations.** As you work through seatmate combinations, ask yourself: Who knows each other already? Who will enjoy getting to know each other? What do the surrounding guests have in common (interests, hobbies, etc.)? Where do they differ in opinions or life experience? What might they talk about?
- **Arrange seating according to the shape or your table.** If you have a rectangular dining table, you, the guest of honor, and/or your most social guest(s) should be seated toward the center of each side. The center seats have the most flexibility to participate in conversations on either side of the table and can easily draw guests' attention. Test out seating couples and plus-ones across from each other so they socialize a bit more with guests. If the table is round, sit couples and plus-ones next to each other.
- **Seat for convenience.** With rectangular tables, the end seats are about convenience. Assign them to someone who may be late or need to leave early, or who has young kids who may call them away from the table. Some hosts also prefer the ends as they may need to slip in and out as the meal progresses. At a round table, the most easily accessible position will be ideal for the host or any parents of small children.

Something from Everyone

When I am preparing for a potluck, I like to create a virtual sign-up sheet so guests can submit their contribution with their RSVP. I make the list visible to everyone so I don't end up with three pies and no proteins. I also like to add a few elements to the sign-up for the friends who don't like to cook—for example, flower arrangements, wine, breads, or ice cream to go with dessert. This encourages guests to lean into their strengths (and helps you cover all the party's needs). On the following pages, my chef friends have graciously shared their recipes for the delicious dishes they brought to the table.

Aretah Ettarh's Pumpkin Seed Salsa Verde

Makes 2½ cups (600 g)

My friend Aretah Ettarh is the chef de cuisine at Gramercy Tavern. Whenever I get to collaborate with Aretah, I know the food will be equal parts delicious and beautiful. For dinner, I prepared a simple roast chicken and Aretah brought some of this delicious pumpkin seed salsa verde as the star accompaniment. The crunchy texture and bright flavor of this salsa verde is really notable with a roast chicken or turkey, but it also elevates something simple like burrata and sourdough. This recipe was made for a *large* gathering with plenty of salsa verde to serve generously over roasted chicken. I also filled mini mason jars for guests to take home. You can easily slim down the yield by reducing all the ingredients by half.

½ cup (85 g) hulled pumpkin seeds

2 cups (480 ml) Colombino extra-virgin olive oil (or your preferred finishing olive oil)

Leaves from 1 bunch parsley, finely chopped

½ bunch chives

Lemon zest

1 teaspoon kosher salt, plus more if needed

Preheat the oven to 300°F (150°C).

Spread the pumpkin seeds on a baking sheet and place them in the oven. Toast for about 10 minutes, until the seeds are golden brown and fragrant. Remove from the oven and let cool completely, about 10 minutes.

Coarsely chop the seeds with a knife or by pulsing them in a food processor. Place the chopped seeds in a fine-mesh sieve and shake gently to remove excess dust, then transfer the seeds to a medium bowl. Add the olive oil, parsley, chives, lemon zest, and salt and stir until well combined.

Taste and season with additional salt if needed, then serve. The salsa verde can be made in advance and stored in an airtight container in the refrigerator for up to 1 week.

Jahvel Fraser's Roasted Veggie Salad

Serves 6

Jahvel Fraser is a private chef and owner of the catering company JVF Pantry based in Queens, New York. Chef Jahvel made sure we had a hearty serving of vegetables with this warm salad, paired perfectly with a tangy vinaigrette.

ROASTED VEGETABLES

2 medium sweet potatoes, peeled and cut into ½-inch (1.3 cm) cubes

2 parsnips, peeled and sliced into ½-inch-thick (1.3 cm) rounds

Kosher salt

4 tablespoons (60 ml) extra-virgin olive oil

8 ounces (225 g) green beans, trimmed

8 ounces (225 g) Brussels sprouts, quartered

8 ounces (225 g) asparagus, ends trimmed

1 small fennel bulb, trimmed, cored, and sliced ¼ inch (6 mm) thick

½ medium red onion, cut into ¼-inch-thick (6 mm) slices

½ teaspoon freshly ground black pepper, plus more if needed

Make the roasted veggies: Preheat the oven to 400°F (200°C).

Place the sweet potatoes on a large rimmed baking sheet and the parsnips on a second. Drizzle each tray with 1 tablespoon of the olive oil and sprinkle with a pinch of salt, then toss. Roast both baking sheets together for about 20 minutes, until the vegetables are tender.

Meanwhile, bring a medium pot of water to a boil over high heat. Fill a large bowl with ice and cold water. Add the green beans to the boiling water and cook until crisp-tender and vibrant green, 1 to 2 minutes. Using a spider, transfer the green beans to the ice bath. Let stand until completely cooled, about 2 minutes. Drain well; pat dry with paper towels.

In a large bowl, combine the Brussels sprouts, asparagus, fennel, onion, and blanched green beans. Toss with the remaining 2 tablespoons olive oil. Season with 1½ teaspoons salt and the pepper.

Remove the sweet potatoes and parsnips from the oven and add half the veggie mixture to each of the baking sheets. Toss until combined and evenly distributed. Place the baking sheets back in the oven and roast for about 8 minutes, until the vegetables are tender and slightly charred. Remove from the oven and let cool to room temperature, about 15 minutes.

VINAIGRETTE

2 tablespoons white balsamic vinegar

1½ teaspoons Dijon mustard

½ small shallot, minced

¼ cup (60 ml) extra-virgin olive oil

¼ teaspoon kosher salt

¼ teaspoon freshly ground black pepper

Meanwhile, make the vinaigrette: In a food processor, combine the vinegar, mustard, and shallot. With the machine running, drizzle in the olive oil and process until emulsified. Season with the salt and pepper.

Assemble the salad: Place the cooled roasted vegetables in a large bowl and toss with the vinaigrette. Taste and season with salt and pepper. Transfer to a serving platter and serve immediately.

Mike Carter's Smoked Short Rib Chili

Serves 12

Chef Mike Carter is known for making one of Philly's best slices of pizza, but his smoked short rib chili is a showstopper that has guests coming back for more and more. Be advised: This dish is a labor of love—it takes more than 4 hours for the flavors to come together.

PICKLED ONIONS

3 cups (720 ml) distilled white vinegar

2 medium red onions, thinly sliced

⅔ cup (155 g) sugar

2 (2-inch/5 cm) knobs fresh ginger, coarsely chopped

3 thyme sprigs

⅓ cup (50 g) kosher salt

CHILI

8 ounces (225 g) dried kidney beans

5 pounds (2.25 kg) bone-in beef short ribs (about 12)

¼ cup (60 ml) liquid smoke

¼ cup (60 ml) soy sauce

2 tablespoons extra-virgin olive oil

1½ teaspoons kosher salt, plus more as needed

½ teaspoon freshly ground black pepper, plus more as needed

Make the pickled onions: In a small pot, bring the vinegar to a boil over medium-high heat. Place the onions, sugar, ginger, thyme, and salt in a large mason jar or quart container. Pour the boiling vinegar into the jar and seal. Swirl the jar to dissolve the sugar and salt. Let stand at room temperature for 1 day, then refrigerate until ready to serve, up to 1 week.

Make the chili: Place the kidney beans in a large bowl, cover with cool water, and let soak at room temperature for 8 hours or up to overnight. Drain and rinse.

Place the short ribs, liquid smoke, and soy sauce in a large bowl. Cover and marinate in the refrigerator for 2 hours or up to overnight.

In a large Dutch oven, heat the olive oil over medium-high heat. Leaving the short ribs in the marinade, season them with the salt and pepper. Working in batches, add the ribs to the Dutch oven and sear, turning occasionally, until browned on all sides, 10 to 12 minutes. Transfer the ribs to a half sheet pan or large plate and repeat with the remaining batches.

Add the onion, garlic, and jalapeño to the Dutch oven and reduce the heat to medium. Cook, stirring occasionally, until the onion is lightly browned and fragrant but not

1 large red onion, finely chopped

3 medium garlic cloves, minced

1 jalapeño, seeded and minced

2 tablespoons tomato paste

3 tablespoons guajillo chile powder

2 tablespoons ancho chile powder

1 tablespoon ground coriander

1 tablespoon ground cumin

1½ teaspoons dried oregano

3 cups (720 ml) red wine, preferably cabernet sauvignon

4 cups (1 L) beef stock

1 (15-ounce/425 g) can crushed tomatoes

FOR SERVING

Cooked rice

Crumbled queso fresco

Chopped fresh cilantro

charred, 5 to 7 minutes. Stir in the tomato paste, guajillo and ancho chile powders, coriander, cumin, and oregano and cook, stirring continuously, until fragrant, about 2 minutes.

Add the wine and cook, stirring and scraping up the browned bits from the bottom of the pot, until the liquid has reduced slightly, about 5 minutes. Add the stock and tomatoes and bring to a simmer.

Return the short ribs and their juices to the Dutch oven. Add the drained kidney beans and bring to a simmer. Reduce the heat to low, cover, and simmer, stirring and skimming fat from the top occasionally, until the beef is fork-tender, 2½ to 3 hours.

Remove the short ribs from the pot and transfer to a large bowl. Remove and discard the bones and fat. Using two forks, shred the meat and return it to the pot. Bring the chili to a simmer and cook, uncovered, until the kidney beans are very tender and the sauce has thickened slightly, about 30 minutes. Taste and season with salt and pepper.

Serve with rice and garnish with queso fresco, pickled onions, and cilantro.

Camari Mick's Tarte Tatin

Serves 10 to 12

Camari Mick is a James Beard Award–nominated pastry chef who understands that the way to the heart is through dessert. She also understands that a store-bought hack is a home cook's friend, so she's adapted her tarte Tatin recipe to include store-bought puff pastry. This dessert is best served warm with multiple scoops of vanilla ice cream.

All-purpose flour, for dusting

1 (14-ounce/370 g) package frozen puff pastry, preferably Dufour brand, thawed

6 or 7 medium apples (such as Granny Smith or Honeycrisp), peeled, halved, and cored

1 tablespoon lemon zest

2 tablespoons fresh lemon juice

½ teaspoon ground cinnamon

½ teaspoon freshly ground black pepper

¼ teaspoon ground allspice

2 teaspoons apple-flavored or unflavored powdered pectin

1 cup (200 g) sugar

4 tablespoons (½ stick/57 g) cold unsalted butter, cut into ½-inch (1.3 cm) cubes

½ vanilla bean pod, split lengthwise and seeds scraped out

Vanilla ice cream, for serving

On a lightly floured surface, roll out the puff pastry until it's about ⅛ inch (3 mm) thick; cut into an 11-inch (28 cm) round. Chill the pastry until ready to use.

Preheat the oven to 375°F (190°C).

In a large bowl, toss the apples with the lemon zest, lemon juice, cinnamon, pepper, and allspice until evenly coated.

In a small bowl, stir together the pectin with some of the liquid from the apple mixture to create a smooth paste. Add the paste to the apples and toss until well coated.

Heat a 10-inch (25 cm) cast-iron skillet over medium-high heat. When the pan is hot, sprinkle about half the sugar evenly over the surface. The sugar should melt instantly. Use a heat-safe rubber spatula to gently stir, while simultaneously sprinkling in the remaining sugar. When all the sugar has melted and turned an amber color, about 3 minutes, reduce the heat to medium-low. Whisk in the cold butter cubes and the vanilla seeds until well combined. Remove from the heat.

Arrange the apples in the skillet in a circular pattern with the cut sides facing up. Pack them tightly, as they will shrink during cooking. Return the skillet to medium-low heat and cook until the apples release their juices and begin to soften and the sauce is bubbling gently, about 20 minutes.

Occasionally baste the apples with the caramel from the bottom of the skillet to infuse them with flavor. Monitor and adjust the heat so the apples cook gently and the caramel does not burn. Remove from the heat.

Drape the puff pastry over the apples, tucking the edges down around the apples inside the skillet. Bake for about 40 minutes, until the puff pastry is golden brown and fully cooked. Remove the skillet from the oven and set it on a wire rack to cool for 15 minutes.

To invert the tart, run a knife around the edge of the skillet to loosen it. Invert a large serving platter over the skillet. Wearing oven mitts, carefully and swiftly flip the skillet and the platter together to transfer the tart to the platter. Be careful; the caramel may be very hot. Let the tart cool for a few more minutes before serving.

Serve warm, with a scoop of vanilla ice cream.

Auzerais Bellamy's German Chocolate Blondies

Serves 12+

Pastry chef Auzerais Bellamy is best known for her moist, chewy dessert bars. Auzerais's German chocolate blondie recipe is for the ambitious home baker who wants to bring a unique dessert to the table to close out a dinner party. As the party creeps into the wee hours of the night, I like to bring out blondies for myself and the other chocolate lovers in the room. Serve these with coffee and tea or another digestif.

BLONDIES

Nonstick cooking spray

½ cup (1 stick/113 g) unsalted butter, at room temperature

1½ cups packed (250 g) dark brown sugar

2 large eggs

1½ cups (180 g) all-purpose flour

3 tablespoons unsweetened cocoa noir or Dutch-processed cocoa powder

1 tablespoon baking powder

1½ teaspoons kosher salt

FROSTING

2½ cups (170 g) sweetened coconut flakes

1½ cups (170 g) pecans

1 (14-ounce/396 g) can sweetened condensed milk

4 large egg yolks

¾ cup (1½ sticks/170 g) unsalted butter, melted

1 teaspoon kosher salt

Make the blondies: Preheat the oven to 325°F (165°C). Spray a 9-by-13-inch (23 by 33 cm) baking pan with nonstick spray. Set aside.

In a large bowl using a handheld mixer, beat the butter and brown sugar together on medium speed until light and fluffy, 3 minutes. Add the eggs one at a time, beating until incorporated after each addition, about 30 seconds total.

In a medium bowl, whisk together the flour, cocoa powder, baking powder, and salt. With the mixer on low speed, gradually add the dry ingredients to the wet ingredients and beat until just combined, about 1 minute.

Using a large offset spatula, spread the batter evenly in the prepared baking pan. Bake for 15 to 18 minutes, until the blondies are set and a toothpick inserted into the center comes out with a few crumbs attached. Remove from the oven (keep the oven on) and immediately press down on the blondies with a flat sheet pan (just to level the blondies, not flatten them). Set the pan on a wire rack and let cool completely, about 30 minutes.

Meanwhile, make the frosting: Line two baking sheets with parchment paper.

Spread the coconut flakes in an even layer over one of the prepared baking sheets; avoid overcrowding. Bake for 5 to 7 minutes, until golden brown and fragrant, stirring every 2 minutes to ensure even color. Keep a close eye—sweetened coconut can brown quickly. Remove from the oven and set aside. Raise the oven temperature to 350°F (175°C).

Place the pecans on the second prepared baking sheet and toast in the oven for about 8 minutes, until they are slightly darker and smell deeply nutty, tossing halfway thorough. Remove from the oven and let cool completely on the pan (they will continue to crisp as they cool). Chop the cooled pecans and set aside.

Bring a medium saucepan of water to a simmer over medium-low heat. In a heatproof medium bowl, whisk together the sweetened condensed milk, egg yolks, and melted butter to combine. Set the bowl over the saucepan, making sure the bottom of the bowl does not touch the water. Cook, stirring often, until the mixture reaches 160°F (70°C). Remove from the heat.

Fold in the pecans, coconut flakes, and salt until coated. Let cool completely, about 30 minutes.

Assemble the blondies: Using a spoon or an offset spatula, spread the frosting evenly over the top of the cooled blondies. Cut into squares and serve. (For an extra-clean cut, pop the blondies in the freezer for 30 minutes before slicing; allow the blondies to return to room temperature before serving.)

Food for Thought

I've found that the best dinner parties coax guests into a state of comfort and openness. Some guests will require a little extra encouragement to really make the most of the time together. When I am hosting, this comes in the form of conversation starters. For larger dinner parties, I like to place a few prepared questions in bowls on the table so guests can reach for them during dinner whenever they are ready, curious, or in need of a conversation change. I find this works best when the questions in the bowl have a shared theme. With this event's proximity to the holiday season and the occupational similarities of the guests, I tied the questions to giving and receiving.

THE SEND-OFF

In my party pantry, I keep a collection of take-home containers so I can send my guests home with leftovers. I also include a custom "House Hewett" sticker, a detail that guests always appreciate. You can create these on Etsy, Canva, and various online platforms.

SEASON:
Winter

GUEST COUNT:
8

PLANNING TIME:
3 weeks

Grown Kid's Birthday Party

FOR CELEBRATING ON A WHIM

When I close my eyes and think about the earliest parties I can remember, I'm flooded with images of childhood birthday parties with cheesy pizzas, even cheesier decorations, and personalized cakes from the local bakery. In my twenties, birthdays were marked with festive dinners, brunches, cocktail parties, and trips. Across my friend groups, these celebrations always gave us something to look forward to and almost always guaranteed that there would be something to look back on and laugh about later.

In celebrating birthdays, we can reclaim our sentiments around age. It is a privilege to get older and to retain fond memories of our youth. I don't remember when it happened, but it felt like I blinked and suddenly my friends and I were getting older, changing careers, finding partners, starting families, and moving to different cities. I suppose this is the beautiful evolution of life, but before I could fully embrace that a new era was at our doorsteps, I wanted just one more night enjoying all the little things that had defined our youth, so I hosted this party for friends from college and friends I had met during my first few years living in the city and working in the entertainment industry.

ON THE MENU

Ordering takeout and staying up late to talk and laugh with my friends is a core memory. Takeout is also a great solution when you want to host but don't want to cook. Just choose your favorite restaurant or local take-out spot and order the items you would be most excited to share. If the party is particularly large, call the restaurant a week prior and see if the order needs to be placed in advance. Schedule takeout to arrive about 30 minutes after the start of the party, so the food is hot just as guests are settled in and ready for dinner. Before guests arrive, you can set out serving platters and utensils so the transfer from the containers to the platters is smooth. For this party, I opted for Chinese takeout, and for dessert I made a chocolate cake and served it with fruit.

Egg rolls

Vegetable dumplings

Beef with broccoli

Pork fried rice

Vegetable lo mein

Sesame chicken

Yellow Cake with
Fudgy Chocolate Buttercream Frosting
(page 184)

Fresh fruit

Sparkling wine

White wine

Water

Sparkling water

IN THE DETAILS

This celebration came together quickly but smoothly thanks to a well-stocked party pantry and takeout. From the pantry, I pulled out streamers, confetti, birthday candles, craft paper, and art supplies, which sparked the idea that the details of this get-together could offer a bit of nostalgia for my guests (and a bit of care for their inner child).

Nostalgic Source Material

I believe a walk down memory lane is good for the soul. In fact, research has found that feelings of nostalgia can increase happiness, boost self-esteem, and foster social connectedness. To evoke this nostalgic feeling at this party, I tapped into a few specific memories that I could share with my guests—including one of coloring place mats at diners with my dad. Inspired by that memory, I set the table with kraft paper and crayons—transforming the entire surface into a blank canvas. It served as both décor and pre-dinner entertainment (and it works for kids and grown kids alike).

PRO TIPS

Bringing Nostalgia to the Party

Tapping into nostalgia is a great way to appreciate the memories we have while creating new ones. The sentiments of nostalgia are especially fun to bring into special occasions like birthdays, anniversaries, and wedding or baby showers. Grab your entertaining journal and write about fond memories. If you are planning the party for someone, ask them to share their memories with you. Jot down notes about food, music, scents, fashion, and activities. Find the themes that feel most interesting to play with for this particular occasion, then transport party guests to a special place and time that is personal to you or the guest of honor. Here are a few areas where you can start *your* walk down memory lane.

- **Food:** A meal, a flavor, or a dessert
- **Music:** A song, an album, a genre, or an era
- **Scents:** An aroma specific to a place or experience
- **Fashion:** An outfit, a trend, or a style
- **Activities:** A craft or a game
- **Entertainment:** A book, a TV show, or a movie

PS: Nostalgia is not an invitation to romanticize time periods or historical events that were harmful to groups of people. Choose your inspiration with care.

Ditch the Beige

I focused on bringing to the event colorful elements that had maximalist energy but required minimal execution. These included confetti, different-colored linen napkins, colorful chopsticks, and streamers. I shared this vision with my local florist, who created small tabletop arrangements with bright-colored wildflowers in bud vases, to save space for coloring and serving platters.

A Good Ol' Days Playlist

At this birthday party, my guests and I had shared our "coming of age" years together. From our college days to our shared big city adventure, these are the songs that kept us dancing between 2008 and 2017.

- **"My House,"** Flo Rida
- **"It's a Vibe,"** 2 Chainz
- **"Party,"** Beyoncé, featuring André 3000
- **"Best Life,"** Cardi B, featuring Chance the Rapper
- **"Workout,"** J.Cole
- **"Feeling Myself,"** Nicki Minaj, featuring Beyoncé
- **"Time of Our Lives,"** Pitbull and Ne-Yo
- **"I Gotta Feeling,"** the Black Eyed Peas
- **"Starships,"** Nicki Minaj
- **"Headlines,"** Drake
- **"Blurred Lines,"** Robin Thicke, featuring T.I. and Pharrell Williams
- **"Young, Wild & Free,"** Snoop Dogg and Wiz Khalifa, featuring Bruno Mars

Serve Takeout on Fine China

The pairing of two things that do not typically go together can spark curiosity and invite guests to step out of their perception about what is "right" or "proper." One of my favorite ways to play with juxtaposition is to serve takeout on what my grandmother would call "the good plates." Combining the inherent casualness of takeout with the formality of fine china, linen napkins, and stemware is a great way to break the "rules."

Takeout & Good Wine

This is always a winning formula (for hosting, for date night in, or when I am just enjoying my own company). When I am shopping for wine, I always tell my local wine shop owner, or caviste, what is on the menu to get their best recommendations. For my Chinese takeout order, they recommended Grüner Veltliner, Torrontes, and Savagnin. These pairings did not disappoint. And because I love the dynamic duo that is takeout and wine, I can also tell you that Chianti and Sangiovese go well with pizza, and dry sparkling wines like Champagne, cava, and crémant are unrivaled for fried chicken. Start keeping track of your favorite bottles and pairings in your entertaining journal.

Yellow Cake

WITH FUDGY CHOCOLATE BUTTERCREAM FROSTING

Serves 12 to 16

I've always had a sweet tooth, and perhaps that's why I love birthday celebrations so much—because I know there will be cake. My favorite is a simple yellow cake that is not too sweet paired with a fudgy chocolate frosting. It's my ideal way to close out a casual yet celebratory occasion.

CAKE

Baking spray

2 cups (250 g) unbleached cake flour

1 teaspoon baking soda

1 teaspoon baking powder, preferably aluminum-free

½ teaspoon kosher salt

½ cup (1 stick/113 g) unsalted butter, at room temperature

1 cup (200 g) granulated sugar

2 large eggs, at room temperature

1 large egg yolk, at room temperature

1 teaspoon pure vanilla extract

12 ounces (340 g) sour cream

Make the cake: Preheat the oven to 350°F (175°C). Spray a 9-by-13-inch (23 by 33 cm) ceramic baking dish with baking spray.

Sift together the cake flour, baking soda, baking powder, and salt into a medium bowl. Set aside.

In the bowl of a stand mixer fitted with the paddle attachment (or in a large bowl using a handheld mixer), cream together the butter and granulated sugar on medium speed until light and fluffy, about 3 minutes.

Add the eggs and egg yolk one at a time, beating well after each addition, about 45 seconds total. Add the vanilla and beat until just combined. Using a rubber spatula, scrape down the sides of the bowl to ensure that the ingredients are fully combined.

With the mixer on low speed, add half the flour mixture, followed by half the sour cream, beating well after each addition, about 1 minute total. Turn off the mixer and use a rubber spatula to scrape down the sides of the bowl. Add the remaining flour mixture and the remaining sour cream. Beat on low until just combined, about 1 minute. Scrape down the sides of the bowl again to ensure that the mixture is fully combined.

Transfer the batter to the prepared baking dish and spread it evenly. Bake for about 25 minutes, until the cake is golden brown and a toothpick inserted into the center comes out clean. Remove from the oven and let cool completely on a wire rack, about 1 hour. (Once cooled, the cake can be frosted in the baking dish.)

CHOCOLATE BUTTERCREAM FROSTING

1 cup (2 sticks/227 g) unsalted butter, cut into ½-inch (1.3 cm) cubes, at room temperature

3 cups (375 g) unsifted confectioners' sugar

1 cup (85 g) unsweetened natural or Dutch-process cocoa powder

⅛ teaspoon kosher salt

1 teaspoon pure vanilla extract

½ cup (120 ml) whole milk

Rainbow sprinkles, for topping (optional)

Meanwhile, make the frosting: In the bowl of a stand mixer fitted with the paddle attachment (or in a large bowl using a handheld mixer), cream the butter on medium speed until light and fluffy, about 3 minutes.

Sift together the confectioners' sugar, cocoa powder, and salt into a small bowl. With the mixer on low speed, add half the dry mixture to the butter and beat until combined, about 30 seconds. Add the vanilla and half the milk; beat until combined, 30 seconds. Turn off the mixer and scrape down the sides of the bowl to ensure that the mixture is fully combined. Add the remaining dry ingredients and milk and beat on low speed until combined, about 30 seconds. Increase the speed to medium and beat until fluffy and lightened in color, about 2 minutes.

Frost the cake: Transfer the cake to a serving platter. Use a spatula or butter knife to spread the frosting over the top. Top with sprinkles, if desired, and enjoy.

Note: I recommend making this cake the day before the celebration. The cake can be frosted the day before or stored in an airtight container to frost the morning of. If storing the frosting in the refrigerator, bring to room temperature before using. The frosted cake can be stored in an airtight container at room temperature for up to 3 days.

Let Them Eat Cake

If it were up to me, every celebration would include cake. For this party, I made a yellow cake with chocolate frosting (and I went heavy on the sprinkles as per the theme). Planning for cake portions and confidence while cake cutting are useful skills to have in your hosting tool kit.

For intimate parties of fourteen or fewer, a 9-inch (23 cm) round cake or 8-inch (20 cm) square cake will be plenty. For larger celebrations (or when you want leftovers), a 9-by-13-inch (23 by 33 cm) half sheet cake will yield 20 to 40 slices. And if you are expecting big celebration energy, an 18-by-26-inch (46 by 66 cm) sheet cake can yield 50 to 80 slices.

In general, a generous slice will be about 2 inches (5 cm), and a more sensible party slice will be 1 inch to 1½ inches (2.5 to 4 cm). Now, I don't expect you to break out a ruler while you are cutting the cake. You can use three fingers to eyeball the size of a generous portion and two fingers to squeeze in more slices. Below is a cake-cutting guide for a 9-by-13 inch (23 by 33 cm) cake, to ensure everyone gets a slice.

Slice Guide for 18 Portions | **Slice Guide for 24 Portions** | **Slice Guide for 54 Portions**

THE SEND-OFF

Favors are best for occasions when guests might bring a gift, like birthday parties, wedding or baby showers, and housewarming parties. See page 218 for my ultimate list of timeless gifts and party favors. Depending on the occasion or theme, you can corral your favors in organza bags, small brown paper bags, pencil cases, small travel totes, or small gift boxes—bonus points if the goody bag is something that can be reused or repurposed. For this occasion, I used Chinese takeout containers and filled them with fortune cookies, thank-you notes, and other small knickknacks, including lip gloss, a key chain, and candy—the final nod to my childhood parties.

POP. FIZZ.
CLINK. DRINK.
MAKE A CHAMPAGNE COCKTAIL
CHAMPAGNE • 4 DASHES OF BITTERS • SUGAR CUBE • GARNISH
MAKE A SPRITZ
ICE • 3 PARTS PROSECCO • 2 PARTS LIQUEUR • 1 PART CLUB SODA (GENTLE STIR) • GARNISH
MAKE A FIZZ
2 PARTS SPIRIT OF CHOICE • 1 PART CITRUS JUICE • A DRIZZLE OF SIMPLE SYRUP • ICE
(SHAKE, SHAKE, SHAKE)
TOP WITH CLUB SODA • GARNISH

SEASON:
Winter

GUEST COUNT:
20+

PLANNING TIME:
5 weeks

Hope & Midnight

FOR GETTING DRESSED UP AND GOING TO THE LIVING ROOM

I believe New Year's Eve is the ultimate celebration of hope. Across time zones, we count down to midnight and embrace the idea that something new (and better) is on the horizon. We encourage that possibility not only with bold resolutions but with rituals of celebration, symbolism, and superstition. My grandmother always had a pot of collard greens and black-eyed peas on the menu for New Year's Day (for good luck and prosperity). My mother always wants the trash out before the New Year arrives.

As you recall your own New Year's Eve traditions, what comes to mind? The manifestations of these traditions may look different from country to country, culture to culture, and even house to house, but what we have in common is hope—and hope is something to celebrate, and to nurture.

Each time you set a goal, pursue it, and celebrate your success with people you love, the seeds of hope are sprouting. With this in mind, I wanted to host a glimmering evening with inspiring company. This party was adults-only, and everyone was invited with a plus-one and a mandate to bring someone who inspires them. This filled the room with both new and familiar faces, the perfect combination when the goal is to create a buzzy atmosphere.

ON THE MENU

For a cocktail party, I approach the menu with a combination of homemade, semi-homemade, and store-bought items. While homemade items are made entirely from scratch, the semi-homemade items utilize ingredients where some of the prep is done for you, and store-bought items of course are things that you pick up ready to serve (or that just require some reheating before serving). I recommend offering two or three options per category, prioritizing menu options that taste good at room temperature or can be heated with minimal fuss as the night goes on. I find that this balance of items makes hosting easier for large or late-night parties where arrival times and appetites will vary throughout the evening.

A Welcome Toast, Three Ways (page 197)

Salad on skewers

French fries

Blini topped with crème fraîche, caviar, and chopped scallions

Shrimp cocktail

Chocolate-covered pretzels

Cream puffs

Mini chocolate tarts

Chocolate mousse dessert bar

A Festive & Fizzy Drink Station (see page 193)

Water and sparkling water

IN THE DETAILS

I wanted this event to be approachably glamorous. In every detail, I wanted my guests to know they deserved the finer things—the fancy food, the nice wine, and a good time. I think New Year's Eve is the perfect occasion to stay up a little too late, laugh a little too loud, and really savor the dawn of a new chapter. I wanted my guests to feel energized by the party's end, and to accomplish that, I turned to caviar, confetti, and lots of bubbly.

Setting an Opulent Scene

In the winter, I look for a bit of decadence in my styling choices. I want details that feel a little lavish and perhaps more worthy of your cold (potentially snowy) trek over to my place. For this, I enjoy mixing metallics (e.g., silver, gold, bronze) and jewel tones. The rich, saturated hues of sapphire, ruby, emerald, and amethyst are quite sensuous together. I brought these colors into the velvet tablecloths and flower arrangements. The shimmer of silver and gold can be spotted in the confetti and tinsel, as well as in the vases, candleholders, and serving platters and bowls. At the stations, acrylic boxes added height variation and dimension—a simple way to bring a more sculptural presentation to an otherwise simple setup. Much like people, individually these details are good, but together, they are sublime. Note: I opt for larger biodegradable confetti pieces for easier cleanup.

PRO TIPS

A Festive and Fizzy Drink Station

At the welcome table, I set up a DIY bubbly bar for guests to make their own welcome drink that would focus on effervescent cocktail favorites. This station served as a natural conversation starter as guests compared which drink and garnish they would chose. A few tips:

- Create a detailed station menu to help guide guests through making a Champagne cocktail, spritz, or fizz.
- Stock the table with juices, specialty syrups, and garnishes to give your guests more options, encouraging their creativity.
- Bring in a few personalized details. I opted for these cocktail napkins printed with "Midnight at the Hewetts'." You might consider custom cups, cocktail stirrers, or edible cocktail toppers.
- Keep a few bottles of sparkling wine, juices, and precut garnishes in the refrigerator for easy replenishment throughout the night.
- Wait to pop the bubbly bottles until guests arrive (for the sake of the bubbles and the moment of spectacle).

An Up Past Midnight Playlist

For New Year's Eve, I wanted the playlist to include a collection of timeless songs that make people want to move and groove.

- **"Life Will Be,"** Cleo Sol
- **"Intimidated,"** Kaytranada, featuring H.E.R.
- **"Rock Your Body,"** Justin Timberlake
- **"24K Magic,"** Bruno Mars
- **"Unforgettable,"** French Montana, featuring Swae Lee
- **"Water,"** Tyla
- **"Work,"** Rihanna, featuring Drake
- **"No Games,"** Serani
- **"It Wasn't Me,"** Shaggy, featuring RikRok
- **"Yeah!"** Usher, featuring Lil Jon and Ludacris
- **"Be Faithful,"** Fatman Scoop, featuring the Crooklyn Clan
- **"Cuff It,"** Beyoncé

A Welcome Toast, Three Ways

Serves 16 to 20

When I am in the kitchen, I love a one-step, two-step. Not everything has to be fancy footwork, and this crostini recipe is the essence of that philosophy. (In fact, I think you should put on a little dance music while you make this one, to get you in the party mood.) Whenever I am hosting a cocktail party or a mix-and-mingle event, I turn to this recipe because it gives people a hearty welcome bite and you can follow one recipe and get options for both meat-eaters and non-meat-eaters since there will be a mushroom, a steak, and a "pantry special" option. This recipe is written to yield about 48 slices in total with about 16 slices of each type. (Note: If you are expecting a few vegans, reduce the whipped goat cheese ingredients by a third and grab a spreadable cashew cheese to use with the pantry special and/or the mushroom toasts.) Be sure to clearly label all options and allergens at the service table.

MUSHROOMS

1 pound (455 g) Baby Bella (cremini) mushrooms, sliced

2 tablespoons extra-virgin olive oil

1 teaspoon kosher salt

¼ teaspoon freshly ground black pepper

CROSTINI

2 (12-inch/30 cm) baguettes, cut on an angle into ½-inch-thick (1.3 cm) slices (about 48 slices total)

3 tablespoons extra-virgin olive oil

½ teaspoon kosher salt

¼ teaspoon freshly ground black pepper

Preheat the oven to 400°F (200°C). Line four baking sheets with parchment paper. (If you don't have enough baking sheets, line those you do have with clean parchment after making each component.)

Make the mushrooms: In a large bowl, toss the mushrooms with the olive oil, salt, and pepper. Spread them in an even layer over one of the prepared baking sheets. Bake for about 20 minutes, until the mushrooms are tender.

Make the crostini: Arrange the baguette slices in a single layer on two of the prepared baking sheets. Brush each slice with the olive oil and season with the salt and pepper on each side. Bake for 4 to 5 minutes, until lightly browned, then flip and bake for another 4 to 5 minutes. Remove from the oven and let cool.

(Continued)

"PANTRY SPECIAL"

½ cup (66 g) lightly salted pistachios, coarsely chopped

STEAK

1 (8-ounce/225 g) hanger steak

1 tablespoon extra-virgin olive oil

¾ teaspoon kosher salt

2 tablespoons unsalted butter

2 large garlic cloves, peeled and quartered

1 rosemary sprig

WHIPPED GOAT CHEESE

16 ounces (455 g) soft goat cheese, at room temperature

1 tablespoon extra-virgin olive oil

FOR SERVING

Balsamic glaze

Fresh thyme leaves

Honey

Flaky sea salt

Make the "pantry special": Spread the nuts evenly over the remaining prepared baking sheet and toast in the oven until lightly browned and fragrant, about 8 minutes. Remove from the oven.

Make the steak: Pat the steak dry with a paper towel. Heat a cast-iron skillet over high heat and add the olive oil. Use a paper towel to pat the steak dry again on both sides, then sprinkle with the salt.

When the pan is just smoking hot, add the steak and sear, undisturbed, until golden brown on the bottom, about 2 minutes. Flip the steak and sear until golden brown on the second side, about 2 minutes. Flip the steak again and add the butter, garlic, and rosemary to the pan. Reduce the heat to medium-high and cook, tilting the skillet and using a spoon to baste the steak with the melted butter, until the steak registers 145°F (63°C) for medium (the steak will continue to cook off the heat). Transfer the steak to a cutting board and let it rest for 5 to 10 minutes.

Meanwhile, make the whipped goat cheese: In the bowl of a stand mixer fitted with the whisk attachment, beat the goat cheese and olive oil on medium speed until creamy, 1 to 2 minutes, scraping down the sides of the bowl with a rubber spatula as needed.

Assemble the toasts: Spread a thin layer of the whipped goat cheese evenly over 16 crostini. Portion some mushrooms on top of the cheese, then drizzle with balsamic glaze and garnish with thyme.

Slice the steak against the grain into 16 slices and place a piece of steak on each of 16 crostini. Garnish with sea salt and thyme.

Top the remaining 16 crostini with the "pantry special" (toasted pistachios), drizzle with honey, and garnish with thyme. Serve immediately.

A Toast to Set the Tone

As the room starts to feel smaller and gentle murmurs become vibrant chatter, it is time to make a toast. My opening toast for this occasion: "Thank you, everyone, for spending the eve of this new year with me. I am grateful for the bonds we share and for this opportunity to gather in celebration of all that is behind us and all that is in front of us. May our pursuits in this New Year continue to fan the flames of hope, passion, and love. Let's raise a glass to the times we've had, the time we're having, and the times we'll have. Cheers!"

"My Drink and My Two-Step"

There is a delicate balance that happens at cocktail parties. As guests maneuver through the party, you can guess with great certainty that one hand will be occupied by a drink. For this reason, I recommend you do two things: (1) Think about the surface areas throughout the party—tables, side tables, counter space—and make sure that guests find a landing spot for their glass. (2) Design your menu to be primarily composed of one-hand, one-bite options. Remember, you want your guests to flow through the party with ease, so be on the lookout for little ways to support their vibing and imbibing.

Station Hopping and Bopping

Throughout the party, food was arranged in stations—including this chocolate mousse bar. Stations naturally encourage guests to move around and explore the party. They are also great icebreakers. I've met some of my favorite people while crowding around a dessert station comparing our topping strategies. More build-your-own-station ideas below.

- Bloody Mary bar
- Bruschetta bar
- Burger or sliders station
- Chili bar
- Hot chocolate bar
- Ice cream sundae bar
- Loaded baked potato bar
- Pancake and/or waffle bar
- Pasta and/or pizza station
- Raw bar (shrimp, oysters, etc.)

THE SEND-OFF

When we choose to have hope, we are attempting to turn our challenges and disappointments into triumphs and art. Before the Champagne bubbles fizzle out, invite your guests to commemorate the evening by writing letters to themselves for the New Year, to end the party on a high note. Set up a station that includes a small sign prompting guests to write down their goals, action steps, and wishes for the life they want in the new year. The station should include note cards, envelopes, pens, and stickers or wax seals to close the envelopes so guests can take them home.

four

The Finer Details

In this section you will find charts, templates, and resources to help you as you work through the planning and hosting of your parties.

A Well-Stocked Pantry & Fridge 206

Guide to Serving Sizes 208

Measurement Conversion Chart 209

Meat Doneness Temperatures 209

A Well-Stocked Home Bar 210

Classic Cocktail Recipes 212

Hiring Event Service Providers 214

Printed Party Papers 217

Timeless Party Favors & Gifts 218

Cleaning Checklist 220

Checklist for Bathroom Toiletries 221

A Well-Stocked Pantry & Fridge

In A Party Planner's Pantry (page 22), I shared a list of kitchen tools, tabletop needs, and party supplies that make home entertaining easier. In this section, you will find a fuller list of tools and ingredients to fully stock your pantry and fridge.

KITCHEN TOOLS

- Baking dishes
- Blender or food processor
- Cake pans, Bundt pans, and loaf pans
- Can opener
- Colander
- Cutting boards
- Dutch oven
- Fine-mesh sieve and spider strainer
- Fire extinguisher
- Fish spatula
- Frying pan (8 to 10 inches/20 to 25 cm)
- Grilling utensils
- Japanese mandoline
- Kitchen scale
- Kitchen scissors
- Kitchen towels
- Knives (chef's, paring, and serrated)
- Ladle
- Measuring cups, liquid and dry
- Measuring spoons
- Microplane grater
- Mixing bowls (stainless steel, various sizes)
- Mortar and pestle
- Pastry brush
- Peeler
- Pepper mill
- Rolling pin
- Saucepans (1 quart/1 L and 4 quarts/4 L)
- Salad spinner
- Sauté pans (with lids, various sizes)
- Silicone spatula
- Spoons (slotted and wooden)
- Stand mixer
- Stockpot (8 to 12 quarts/8 to 12 L)
- Thermometer for meat and poultry
- Tongs (various sizes)
- Whisks (various sizes)
- Wire racks

SHELF-STABLE INGREDIENTS

- All-purpose flour
- Baking powder
- Baking soda
- Beans
- Black peppercorns
- Canned crushed tomatoes
- Cocoa powder, unsweetened
- Coffee
- Cooking oils (avocado oil, grapeseed oil, safflower oil)
- Cornmeal
- Cornstarch
- Crackers (various types)
- Dark bar chocolate, 70% cocoa
- Dijon mustard
- Dried fruits (apricots, figs, mangoes)
- Dried pasta (elbow pasta, penne rigate, spaghetti)
- Evaporated milk
- Extra-virgin olive oils (regular for cooking and for sauces/dips, and infused for added flavor)
- Extracts (almond, lemon, vanilla)
- Fruit preserves (apricot, fig, raspberry, strawberry)
- Honey
- Hot honey
- Hot sauce
- Ketchup
- Maple syrup
- Nuts (almonds, cashews, pecans, walnuts)
- Quinoa
- Rice (basmati, brown, jasmine, risotto)
- Salts (Diamond Crystal kosher salt, fine sea salt, and flaky sea salt)
- Steel-cut oats
- Snacks (popcorn, pretzels, veggie chips)
- Spices (allspice, bay leaves, cayenne, cloves, cumin, curry powder, granulated garlic, granulated onion, ground cinnamon and cinnamon sticks, nutmeg, oregano, red pepper flakes, smoked paprika)
- Soy sauce
- Stocks (chicken and/or vegetable)
- Sugars (confectioners', dark brown, granulated, light brown)
- Teas (assorted)
- Tomato sauce
- Vinegars (apple cider, balsamic, distilled white, red wine)
- Worcestershire sauce
- Yeast
- Yellow mustard

PRODUCE AND PERISHABLES

- Butter
- Carrots
- Celery
- Cheeses (blue cheese, mild and sharp cheddars, goat cheese, mozzarella, Parmigiano-Reggiano, Pecorino Romano)
- Citrus (lemons, limes, oranges)
- Eggs
- Fresh herbs (basil, cilantro, mint, parsley, rosemary, sage, thyme)
- Fresh fruit (whatever is in season)
- Garlic
- Ginger
- Mayonnaise
- Milk and creamer
- Onions
- Scallions
- Shallots
- Sour cream

Guide to Serving Sizes

CATEGORY	AMOUNT PER PERSON
Appetizers	
Canapés	4
Charcuterie	2 ounces (55 g) cheese 2 ounces (55 g) meat 4 to 6 crackers or slices of bread
Beverages	
Beer	1 (12-ounce/355 ml) bottle every half an hour
Cocktails	2 drinks in the first hour and 1 drink per additional hour
Coffee and tea	1 to 2 servings
Ice	½ pound (225 g)
Punch	3 cups
Soft drinks and sparkling water	2 drinks in the first hour and 1 drink per additional hour
Water	16 ounces (480 ml)
Wine	½ bottle
Main Dishes	
Meat, poultry, and seafood	4 to 6 ounces (115 to 170 g)
Pasta	2 to 3 ounces (57 to 85 g) dry pasta (or 1 cup/140 g cooked)
Soup	2 cups (480 ml)
Sides	
Beans, grains, and potatoes	½ cup (75 g)
Bread	1 or 2 slices or rolls
Pasta salad, coleslaw, and potato salad	½ cup (120 g)
Salad	½ cup (40 g)
Vegetables	½ cup (90 g)
Dessert	
Cake	1 layer cake for every 10 to 12 guests
Cookies	2 or 3
Fruit salad	½ cup (125 g)
Ice cream, sorbet, and gelato	1 cup (150 g)
Pie or tart	1 (9-inch/23 cm) pie or tart for every 5 guests

Measurement Conversion Chart

A pinch	⅛ teaspoon		
1 teaspoon			5 ml
3 teaspoons	1 tablespoon	½ fluid ounce	15 ml
2 tablespoons		1 fluid ounce	
¼ cup	4 tablespoons	2 fluid ounces	60 ml
1 cup	½ pint	8 fluid ounces	240 ml
2 cups	1 pint	16 fluid ounces	480 ml
4 cups	1 quart	32 fluid ounces	1 L
16 cups	1 gallon	128 fluid ounces	4 L

Meat Doneness Temperatures

Fish		145°F (63°C)
Poultry		165°F (74°C)
Pork	Medium	140–145°F (60–63°C)
Brisket		195–205°F (90–96°C)
Beef, Lamb, Veal	Rare	120–125°F (49–52°C)
	Medium-Rare	130–135°F (54–57°C)
	Medium	140–145°F (60–63°C)
	Medium-Well	150–155°F (65–68°C)
	Well-Done	160–165°F (71–74°C)

A Well-Stocked Home Bar

A well-stocked bar can keep a party going. In curating my home bar, my aim was to have the essentials for crafting classic cocktails, as well as a few fun tools and ingredients. Here is a list to make sure your bar is prepared for spontaneous and spirited hosting.

- ❑ Alcohol (choose two or three from among these options: gin, rum, tequila, vodka, and whiskey)
- ❑ Alcohol alternatives (like Seedlip, Aplós, Curious Elixirs, Pentire Adrift, and Wilfred's)
- ❑ Bitters
- ❑ Bottle opener
- ❑ Bottle stoppers
- ❑ Citrus juicer
- ❑ Cocktail charms (to help guests keep track of their glasses)
- ❑ Cocktail napkins
- ❑ Cocktail shaker
- ❑ Cocktail stirring spoons
- ❑ Corkscrew
- ❑ Decanters
- ❑ Glassware (cocktail, highball, martini, or preferred specialty glasses)
- ❑ Hawthorne strainer
- ❑ Ice buckets and tongs
- ❑ Ice trays and specialty ice molds
- ❑ Jiggers (for cocktails)
- ❑ Lemons and limes
- ❑ Liqueurs (these come in a variety of flavors; on my cart: Campari, Cointreau, Grand Marnier, St-Germain, and a crème de cassis)
- ❑ Maraschino cherries
- ❑ Mixing glasses (for cocktails)
- ❑ Muddler (for cocktails)
- ❑ Olives
- ❑ Stirrers
- ❑ Straws (agave or other biodegradable option)
- ❑ Simple syrup
- ❑ Sodas and seltzers
- ❑ Wine (red, rosé, sparkling, white)

TEN TO ONE
CARIBBEAN WHITE RUM
45% ALC. BY VOL. (90 PROOF)
1827
Grand Marnier
-LIQUEUR-
MADE WITH COGNAC AND ORANGE LIQUEUR
PARIS

Classic Cocktail Recipes

This chart covers the basics. Don't be afraid to remix these recipes by adding seasonal twists or fanciful details to match the occasion.

DRINK	SPIRIT	INGREDIENTS		GLASS	DIRECTIONS	GARNISH
Daiquiri	2 ounces (60 ml) white rum	1 ounce (30 ml) fresh lime juice	½ ounce (15 ml) simple syrup	Cocktail glass	Pour the ingredients into a cocktail shaker, add ice, and shake until well chilled. Strain into the glass. Garnish and serve.	Lime slice
Manhattan	2 ounces (60 ml) rye whiskey	1 ounce (30 ml) sweet vermouth	2 dashes Angostura bitters	Nick & Nora or coupe glass	Pour the ingredients into a mixing glass, add ice, and stir until well chilled. Strain into the Nick & Nora or coupe glass. Garnish and serve.	Lemon twist
Margarita	2 ounces (60 ml) blanco tequila	1 ounce (30 ml) fresh lime juice + ½ ounce (15 ml) orange liqueur	½ ounce (15 ml) agave syrup	Rocks glass	Pour the ingredients into a cocktail shaker, add ice, and shake until well chilled. Rim the rocks glass with salt or sugar and fill it with fresh ice. Strain the cocktail into the glass. Garnish and serve.	Kosher salt or sugar, for rimming the glass + lime wheel
Martini	2½ ounces (75 ml) gin	½ ounce (15 ml) dry vermouth	1 dash orange bitters	Cocktail glass	Pour the ingredients into a mixing glass, add ice, and stir until well chilled. Strain into the glass. Garnish and serve.	Lemon twist
Mint Julep	2 ounces (60 ml) bourbon	8 mint leaves	½ ounce (15 ml) simple syrup	Julep cup or rocks glass	In the julep cup or rocks glass, muddle the mint leaves and simple syrup. Add the bourbon and fill the cup or glass with crushed ice. Stir well. Slap the mint sprig on the back of your hand to release the oils and aromas, garnish the cup or glass, and serve.	Mint sprig

DRINK	SPIRIT	INGREDIENTS		GLASS	DIRECTIONS	GARNISH
Mojitos	2 ounces (60 ml) white rum	3 mint leaves + ½ ounce (15 ml) simple syrup	¾ ounce (22 ml) fresh lime juice + club soda to top	Highball glass	In a shaker, muddle the mint leaves and simple syrup. Add the rum, lime juice, and ice. Fill the glass with ice, then shake and strain the cocktail into the glass. Top with club soda. Garnish and serve.	Mint sprig + lime wheel
Moscow Mule	2 ounces (60 ml) vodka	½ ounce (15 ml) fresh lime juice	3 ounces (90 ml) ginger beer	Mule mug or highball glass	Fill the mug or glass with ice and add the vodka and lime juice. Stir and top with the ginger beer. Garnish and serve.	Lime wheel
Negroni	1 ounce (30 ml) gin	1 ounce (30 ml) Campari	1 ounce (30 ml) sweet vermouth	Rocks glass	Pour the ingredients into a mixing glass, add ice, and stir until well chilled. Strain into the rocks glass and add a large ice cube. Garnish and serve.	Orange peel
Old-Fashioned	2 ounces (60 ml) bourbon	1 teaspoon sugar + 1 teaspoon water	3 dashes Angostura bitters	Rocks glass	In a mixing glass, stir the sugar and water together until the sugar is dissolved. Add the bourbon, bitters, and ice and stir until well chilled. Strain into the rocks glass and add a large ice cube. Garnish and serve.	Orange twist
Sidecar	1½ ounces (45 ml) cognac	¾ ounce (22 ml) orange liqueur	¾ ounce (22 ml) fresh lemon juice	Cocktail glass	Pour the ingredients into a shaker, add ice, and shake until well chilled. Rim the cocktail glass with sugar and strain the cocktail into the glass. Garnish and serve.	Sugar, for rimming the glass + orange twist
Tom Collins	2 ounces (60 ml) dry gin	1 ounce (30 ml) fresh lemon juice + ½ ounce (15 ml) simple syrup	Club soda to top	Highball glass	Pour the gin, lemon juice, and simple syrup into the glass. Fill with ice, top with club soda, and stir. Garnish and serve.	Lemon wheel + maraschino cherry

Hiring Event Service Providers

Refer to this chart when contacting local service providers for your event needs. For all service providers, request a detailed contract that outlines payment structures, cancellation policies, and other booking requirements.

SERVICE PROVIDER	INFORMATION THEY WILL NEED	QUESTIONS TO ASK
Private Chef or Caterer	• Occasion • Event date and time • Location • Guest count • Menu vision and special requests • Details about cooking and prep space(s) • Budget	• What are some of your most popular menus or menu items? Are you open to customized menus? • Can your menus accommodate dietary restrictions and allergies? • How much kitchen staff and waitstaff will accompany you for this event? • Do you have a children's menu (if applicable)? • When are final menu selections and guest count due? • How much time do you need for setup and breakdown? • How will you handle cleanup, dishwashing, and trash removal?
Rental Company	• Occasion • Event date and time as well as date(s) and times for delivery and pickup • Location • Desired items and quantities • Instructions for delivery and/or pickup	• Can your delivery crew set up tables and chairs if a floor plan is provided? • How would you like used plateware, linens, or other rental items to be packed up for return?
Florist	• Occasion • Event date and time as well as setup and pickup time • Location • Floral needs (including table dimensions or other placements) • Any theme, color, or styling that will fit the event • Budget	• Can you provide a proposal with example of flowers and vases? • How much time do you need for setup? • Will you return to pick up the vases after the event?

SERVICE PROVIDER	INFORMATION THEY WILL NEED	QUESTIONS TO ASK
Musician(s)	• Occasion • Event date and time • Location • Guest count • Entertainment vision and special requests • Details about the performance space (size of space, inside or outside, nearest outlet, etc.) • Details about the schedule of the event	• Do you have experience performing at events of this nature? • Are you open to song requests or do you have a list of songs we must choose from? • What equipment do you bring? What does the host need to provide? • Do your instruments or equipment need to be close to an outlet or lighting source?
DJ	• Occasion • Event date and time • Location • Guest count • Entertainment vision and special requests • Details about your entertaining space (size of space, inside or outside, nearest outlet, etc.) • Details about the schedule of the event	• Do you have experience performing at events of this nature? • What is your style? Do you stick to a particular genre of music, or do you have an open format? (An "open format" typically means they are open to playing all genres.) • Are you able to incorporate my music direction or song requests? • Can you bring all your own equipment?
Activity Planner, Providers of Guided Experiences, and Performers	• Occasion • Event date and time • Location • Guest count • Entertainment vision and special requests • Details about your entertaining space (size of space, inside or outside, nearest outlet, etc.) • Details about the schedule of the event	• How many people from your staff will be needed for this event? • Do you need access to water, power, or Wi-Fi for this experience? • How much space do you need? • How will you handle cleanup post event (if applicable)?
Photographer and/or Videographer	• Occasion • Event date and time • Location • Guest count • Reference photos and special requests • Details about the schedule of the event • Shot list	• What is the turnaround time for the final photos or video(s)? • Will you do light retouching to the photographs? • Do you have similar events in your portfolio? • What file formats will be delivered?

Spencer

for dinner

aretah's fancy fowl

jahvel's roasted vegetable salad

mike's short rib chili

for dessert

auzerais' german chocolate blondies

camari's apple tarte tatin

vanilla ice cream

Printed Party Papers

When it comes to parties, there are lots of paper goods—signage, menus, place cards, labels, cocktail napkins—and how you select and design these will give your party personality.

SIGNAGE & MENUS

For casual gatherings, a piece of craft paper and a Sharpie will get the job done. Just write them out and place them on the table or tack them to the wall. For occasions that require a bit more detail or a design that adheres to a theme, you have a few options: For small gatherings, you can pick up beautiful stationery at Paper Source or your local stationery shop and handwrite them. For larger gatherings, you can design your signage and menus on a website like Canva and have them printed. If the occasion is extra special, you can order custom items on sites like Minted or Etsy.

PAPER NAPKINS & PERSONALIZED LABELS

You may have noticed in Part III that my parties often have themed cocktail napkins and other personalized details. I find themed paper napkins at a local party supply shop and order personalized napkins, labels, and other details on sites like Etsy, Minted, and Paper Source.

PLACE CARDS

The previous options for signage and menus also apply to simple tented place cards. If you are hosting large gatherings often, I recommend keeping a few of these in your party pantry, so you always have them at the ready. But place cards can be as creative and personal as you would like them to be. Here are a few more ideas for displaying names in a way that complements your tablescape or theme:

- Fruit (names written on whole pieces or attached to dried slices)
- Leaves, petals, pine cones, shells, or other theme-related objects
- Tags tied with ribbon (or write the names directly on thicker ribbons)
- Photographs or illustrations of guests
- Small engraved or personalized gifts
- Wine corks

Timeless Party Favors & Gifts

- Artisanal packaged food
- Bar of scented soap
- Candy with custom wrappers
- Custom matchbooks
- Desserts like macarons, cookies, or mini pies (bonus points if they're gifted on a beautiful vintage plate or in special packaging)
- Dried fruit cocktail garnishes (e.g., citrus wheels, dragon fruit slices, apple slices)
- Flour mix (i.e., the dry ingredients for pancakes, cookies, or fried chicken)
- Flowers (send guests home with a few stems from the arrangements)
- Fresh herbs or dried herbs (in a beautiful pouch)
- Gilded or custom playing cards
- Hand fans
- Hand soap and lotion set (look for something natural, beautifully packaged, and with a seasonally appropriate scent)
- Handwritten thank-you note
- Homemade granola
- Iron-on patches
- Olive oil and vinegar set
- Polaroid picture (capture guests throughout the event and send them home with their photo)
- Puzzle
- Seed packets
- Souvenir spoons
- Specialty coffee (ground) or tea (loose leaf or bags)
- Specialty honey
- Vintage ashtray
- Vintage candy tin (fill with mints or specialty chocolates)
- Wine (bonus: use a white paint pen or a black Sharpie to write a brief toast or note)

Gifting as a Guest

Being a great host also means being a great guest. When you are attending a party, always consider bringing a gift, contribution, or small token to thank the host for their hospitality. If you want to give the host flowers, be sure to bring them in a vase, so the flowers can be placed without a fuss.

WITH LOVE FROM HOUSE HEWETT
for you

Cleaning Checklist

ENTRY

- ❑ Exterior: Sweep the front porch, steps, and walkway
- ❑ Interior: Dust, vacuum, and mop
- ❑ Tidy the coat closet and make sure you have enough hangers

KITCHEN

- ❑ Clean out the refrigerator and wipe down the shelves
- ❑ Tuck small appliances away for more counter space
- ❑ Clean the kitchen counters, table, sink, and cooktop
- ❑ Sweep and mop

LIVING ROOM AND DINING ROOM

- ❑ Declutter and dust surfaces
- ❑ Vacuum and lint roll upholstered furniture
- ❑ Fluff sofa cushions and pillows
- ❑ Vacuum and mop

BATHROOM

- ❑ Declutter bathroom cabinets and drawers
- ❑ Check stock of hand soap, lotion, toilet paper, and other toiletries (see opposite)
- ❑ Scrub the sink, toilet, and shower/tub, and wipe down the mirror and counters
- ❑ Hang fresh hand towels
- ❑ Sweep and mop

OUTDOOR SPACE

- ❑ Sweep
- ❑ Wipe down outdoor furniture

Checklist for Bathroom Toiletries

THE BASICS

- ❏ Air freshener or fragrance
- ❏ Hand sanitizer
- ❏ Hand soap
- ❏ Hand towels
- ❏ Lotion
- ❏ Tissues
- ❏ Toilet paper

TO REFRESH

- ❏ Floss picks
- ❏ Mints
- ❏ Mouthwash with mini paper cups
- ❏ Menstrual products
- ❏ Bobby pins
- ❏ Hair ties
- ❏ Lint roller
- ❏ Safety pins
- ❏ Stain remover

TO REAPPLY

- ❏ Bug repellant
- ❏ Deodorant spray
- ❏ Sunscreen

FIRST AID

- ❏ Antihistamine
- ❏ Antiseptic wipes
- ❏ Antacids
- ❏ Antibiotic ointment
- ❏ Bandages
- ❏ Hydrogen peroxide
- ❏ Eye drops
- ❏ Pain relievers

AFTERWORD

EVERYTHING I'VE LEARNED ABOUT LIFE (SO FAR) WHILE ENTERTAINING

After every party, I take out my entertaining journal and jot down a few notes. I include the things that worked well. The things that did not work so well. And the little stories and reflections I want to carry with me. This after party journaling ritual has carried me through many years, many celebrations, and even a few tears. Below are ten entries that I return to most. I hope they bring you encouragement as you venture off on your own hosting journey.

1. If you want to be good at anything, make it a habit and your confidence will grow. If you want to throw great parties, start by making hosting a habit.
2. Ask for help. With dinner, with the setup, with the dishes, and with life.
3. How it feels will always be more important than how it looks.
4. Choose freedom over perfection.
5. If all else fails, you can always order takeout.
6. Keep some cookie dough in the freezer for emergencies.
7. Follow your plan, not your mood. Some days you might not wake up feeling confident, motivated, or celebratory. In these moments, having joy-filled routines and rituals will help you push through.
8. It's not about how long the party (or this life) will last. It's about what we do with our time together.
9. Parties remind us that all good things come to an end. Even parties that are exciting, full of love, and bustling with energy must wax and wane, and eventually fizzle out. You can leave yourself in the wake of life's endings sad, disappointed, and broken. Or you can begin again. You can try again. You can love again. And you can always throw another party.
10. Finally, and most important, take every opportunity you have to gather with people you love, be present, and celebrate your sometimes messy but always beautiful life.

Happy hosting!

Amber

Be hospitable to one another without grumbling.

—1 Peter 4:9
(New King James Version)

FURTHER READING

FOR INSPIRATION & INFORMATION

The Art of Gathering: How We Meet and Why It Matters by Priya Parker

B. Smith: Rituals & Celebrations by Barbara Smith

Hill House Living: The Art of Creating a Joyful Life by Paula Sutton

The Martha Manual: How to Do (Almost) Everything by Martha Stewart

Wine Pairing for the People: The Communion of Wine, Food, and Culture from Africa and Beyond by Cha McCoy with Layla Schlack

Wine Simple by Aldo Sohm and Christine Muhlke

FOR RECIPES

Apéritif: Cocktail Hour the French Way by Rebekah Peppler

Cheryl Day's Treasury of Southern Baking by Cheryl Day

The Food Lab: Better Home Cooking Through Science by J. Kenji López-Alt

Jubilee: Recipes from Two Centuries of African American Cooking by Toni Tipton-Martin

Juke Joints, Jazz Clubs & Juice: Cocktails from Two Centuries of African American Cookbooks by Toni Tipton-Martin

Salt, Fat, Acid, Heat: Mastering the Elements of Good Cooking by Samin Nosrat

The Taste of Country Cooking by Edna Lewis

Vibration Cooking, or The Travel Notes of a Geechee Girl by Vertamae Smart-Grosvenor

Watermelon and Red Birds: A Cookbook for Juneteenth and Black Celebrations by Nicole A. Taylor

ACKNOWLEDGMENTS

IT TAKES A VILLAGE TO PLAN A PARTY

Join me in raising a glass . . .

To my party people, Sunny Dae, Rashida Zagon, Clay Williams, Hip Torres, Xiana Gutierrez, Jahvel Fraser, Jillian Atkinson, Aretah Ettarh, Camari Mick, Mike Carter, Auzerais Bellamy, Mia Taylor, Alia Hodge, Athena Partington, Thérèse Nelson, Jasmin Coates, Jasmine Smith, Gabby Babson, Nana Akua Asante, and Zorah Hall for being part of the party that was conceiving, writing, editing, and compiling this book. And an extra *cin cin* to my agents, Monica Odom and Shabnam Banerjee-McFarland, who helped make this dream a reality.

To my editor, Bridget Monroe Itkin, and the entire Artisan team: Lia Ronnen, Zach Greenwald, Hillary Leary, Ivy McFadden, Sibylle Kazeroid, Julia Perry, Joan Shapiro, Annie O'Donnell, Shubhani Sarkar, Nina Simoneaux, Suet Chong, Donna Brown, Moira Kerrigan, and MacKenzie Collier. I am beyond grateful for your support, diligence, and collaboration in making this book bigger and better (and more beautiful) than anything I could have imagined.

To my parents, who taught me to lead with love, to trust God, to work hard, and to always come home for the holidays. To Spencer and Asia, for being my constant confidants. To my in-laws, Wayne, Simonne, Morgan, and Graeme, who cheered me on at every step. And to my entire family, who make sure every get-together roars with laughter and joy. My love for parties flows from you all.

To Alexandria, Shareese, Fatou, Cathy, Little Amber, Brittany, Shannon, Josh, Ashoka, Morgan, Steph, Nabeela, Imani, Eric, Khalid, Skylar, Kaitlyn, Jodi-Lee, Brian, and Michael, for every hug, every prayer, every word of endearment, and every RSVP. Thank you.

To Jordan, my forever plus-one. I've been about you. I'm still about you. And I'm always going to be about you. Thank you for committing to a lifetime of hosting with me. Love you, always.

INDEX

NOTE: Page references in italics refer to figures and photos.

A

activity-based gatherings, 43, 50
activity planner, 215
after-party reflections, 84, 223
Alston, Wendell "DJ," 157
apéritif, 96

B

birthday party for grown-ups, 174–187
 about, 175
 cake recipe and portioning, 184–186
 colorful elements, 180, *180–181*
 on the menu, 176–177
 nostalgia, evoking, 178–179
 playlist for, 181
 the send-off, 187
 takeout for, 182–183
block parties, 43, 50

C

cake-decorating craft party, 110–123
 about, 43, 111
 craft club types, 122
 crudités platter, *112–113*, 118
 décor for, 114
 on the menu, 112–113, 119
 playlist for, 120
 the send-off, 123
 supplies for, 115–116
cakes, about, 123, 186
cakes, recipes, 36, 184–185
candles/candlelight, 27, 63, 92, 160
casual gatherings, 32, 57, 85
charcuterie board, 148, *149*
checklists
 for cleaning, 220
 final prep timeline, 80–81
 for guest experience, 77
 invitation details, 51
 overnight guests, 33
 pre-party tasks, 78
cleaning, 78, 84, 85, 131, 220, 221
cocktails. *see* wine and spirits
color, 65, 95, 116, 128, 180, 192. *see also* décor
communal meals, 43, 50
conversation, 66, 71–73, 83, 85, 172, 193
cookouts, 124–139
 about, 43, 125
 alfresco décor, 128–129
 chilled beverages, 132–133
 entertaining across generations, 128
 format of, 43
 games for, 138
 grilling tips, *130*, 131
 invitations for, 50
 on the menu, 126–127
 playlist for, 136
 recipes, 132–135
 the send-off, 139
craft parties. *see* cake-decorating craft party
crudités platter, 118

D

décor
 for birthday party, 178
 budgeting for, 53
 centerpieces, 27
 as conversation starter, 66, 193
 for cookouts, 128–129
 for craft party, 114
 lighting and, 63
 for New Year's party, 192
 sensory experiences, 31
 tips on, 66
design and atmosphere, 62–67
desserts
 post-dessert linger, 108
 recipes, 106–107, 168–169, 170–171, 184–185
 in winding down party, 84
dinner parties, 11–12, 40, 42, 49

E

entertaining journal. *see* journaling

F

favors, 53, 57, 84, 109, 187, 218, *219*
flowers
 budgeting for, 53
 colorful, 180, *180–181*
 design and, 66
 as gift to host, 218
 hiring florists, 214
 selecting/arranging, *94*, 95
 vases/accessories, 27
flow in entertaining space, 62, *62*, 201

food and drink. *see also* recipes; wine and spirits; *individual types of parties*
  beverage options, 61
  budgeting for, 53
  hiring chef/caterer, 60, 214
  labeling/signage, 35, 119, 197, 217
  menu-planning, 59, 77
  sensory experiences of, 31
  serving sizes, 208
  shopping and stocking, 78
  takeout, 60, 177, 182, 183
fragrance, 31

G

game night, 140–153
  about, 43, 141
  charcuterie board, 148, *149*
  on the menu, 142–143
  organizing tips, 145
  playlist for, 150
  the send-off, 153
  setting the rules, 144
  snacks and drinks, 146–147
  wrapping up, 152
games/activities, 28, 74, 138
gifts, 84, 85, 218
guests
  in building playlists, 70
  considering needs of, 51, 59
  guest experience checklist, 77
  host gifts, 84, 218
  introductions, 83
  list and invitations, 45, 47–51
  overnight guests, 33–37
  potluck sign-up, 162
  RSVPs, 50, 51, 145, 155
  special gestures for, 57
  unexpected guests, 85

H

Hewett, Amber Mayfield, 9, *10*
hiring service providers, 60, 61, 70, 78, 84, 214–215
home preparations, 18–37
  everyday hosting, 32
  mindset of host, 20–21, 83
  overnight guests, 33–37
  sensory experiences, 31
  well-stocked pantry, 22–29
host gifts, 218
hosting parties. *see also* guests; *individual types of parties*
  art of hosting, 83–84
  author reflections, 11–14
  home preparations, 18–37
  planning, 38–85
  resources and lists, 204–221. *see also* checklists
  types of parties, 86–203

I

intentional planning, 40–41, 42, 52, 65
invitations, 49–51

J

journaling
  about entertaining journal, 17, 28
  after-party reflections, 84, 223
  for casual gathering, 32
  in evoking nostalgia, 179
  on favorite wine pairings, 183
  on guests' needs, 51, 128
  on hosting style, 21
  for intention setting, 41
  on seating plans, 161
  on space and flow, 62, *62*
Juneteenth, 125, 133

K

Kaikai, Jenneh, 115
kid-friendly parties, 77
kitchen tools, 24, 206

L

labeling/signage, 35, 119, 173, 197, 217
l'apéro (apéritif), 96
lighting, 63
lists. *see* checklists

M

measurement conversion chart, 209
meat doneness temperatures, 209
menu-planning, 59, 77. *see also individual types of parties*
mix and mingle gatherings, 43, 50
mood boards, 55
music
  budgeting for, 53
  hiring DJ/musician, 70, 215
  playlists, 31, 100, 120, 136, 150, 158, 181, 194
  playlists, building, 68, 70, 78
  volume control, 69

N

New Year's Eve parties, 188–203
  about, 189
  design for ease and flow, *200–201*, 201
  DIY beverage station, 193, *193*
  food stations, 202, *202*
  on the menu, 190–191, 197–198
  opulent color and details, 192, *192*
  playlist for, 194
  the send-off, 203
  toast for, 199, *199*
nostalgia, 178–179

O

overnight guests, 33–37

P

pantry
  birthday decorations, 178
  leftover containers, 28, 173
  pre-party inventory, 78
  stocking, 22–29, 206–207
  Sunday supper staples, 92
paper goods. *see* partyware
party types, 86–203
  birthday party for grown-ups, 174–187
  cookout, 124–139
  crafting (cake decorating), 110–123

party types *continued*
deciding on type, 42
friendsgiving potluck, 154–173
game night, 140–153
New Year's Eve, 188–203
party formats, 43
Sunday supper, 88–109
partyware
budgeting for, 53
paper goods/accessories, 28
personalized, 173, 193, 217
printed papers, 217
personal style of host, 20–21
photographer, hiring, 215
planning techniques, 38–85
art of hosting, 83–84
atmosphere and design, 62–67
checklists, 77–81. *see also* checklists
choosing date and time, 44
common dilemmas, 85
deciding on party type, 42–43. *see also* party types
food and drink, 59–61. *see also* food and drink
guest lists and invitations, 47–51
intentional planning, 40–41, 52
music and entertainment, 68–75
priorities and budgeting, 45, 52–53
timelines, 45, 80–81
visualizing your party, 54–57
playlists. *see* music
potlucks, 154–173
conversation starters, 172
friendsgiving, 155
guest sign-up for, 60, 162
on the menu, 156–157
playlist for, 158
recipes, 163–171
seating plan, 161
the send-off, 173
table décor, 160
produce/perishables, 207

R

recipes
Auzerais Bellamy's German Chocolate Blondies, 170–171
Camari Mick's Tarte Tatin, 168–169
Mike Carter's Smoked Short Rib Chili, 166–167
classic cocktails, 212–213
Coffee Cake, 36, *37*
Dinner Party Pasta, 104–105
Aretah Ettarh's Pumpkin Seed Salsa Verde, *162*, 163
Jahvel Fraser's Roasted Veggie Salad, 164–165
Camari Mick's Tarte Tatin, 168–169
Peach Galette, 106–107
Red Berry Salad, *134*, 135
Red Drink, *132*, 133
The Salad Is a Spectacle, 102–103
Vermouth Pitcher Spritzer, *96*, 97
Welcome Bread Board with Party Thyme Dip, *98*, 99
A Welcome Toast, Three Ways, *196*, 197–198
Yellow Cake with Fudgy Chocolate Buttercream Frosting, 184–185
rental company, 214
rituals/traditions, 12–14, 32–33, 91, 92, 108, 133, 155, 189, 223

S

salad recipes, 102–103, 135, 164–165
Scott, Emily, 160
seating, 77, 161, *161*
sensory experiences, 31
serving sizes, 208
serving tools, 26
shelf-stable ingredients, 207
signs. *see* labeling/signage
Sunday supper, 88–109
about, 89
after-dinner linger, 108
appetizers and drink, 96–99
flower arranging, 95
on the menu, 90–91
playlist for, 100
recipes, 97–99, 102–107
the send-off, 109
table-setting, 92–93
supper club, 11–14, 40

T

table-settings, 92–93, 160
tableware, 25
takeout food, 60, 177, 182, 183
thank-you notes, 28, 84
timelines for party, 44–45, 80–81
toasts. *see also* wine and spirits
during game night, 144, 152
for New Year's Eve, 199
opening with, 83
To Be Hosted (supper club), 11–14, 40
toiletries, 33, 53, 78, 221
touch and textures, 31, 66, 116
traditions. *see* rituals/traditions

V

visualizing your party, 54–57

W

weather, 59, 77
winding down a party, 84
wine and spirits
getting home safely, 85
New Year's DIY bar, 193
potluck selections, 157
pre-party inventory, 78
recipes, 97, 133, 212–213
takeout food pairings, 183
variety of options, 61
well-stocked home bar, 210

Xiana Gutierrez

AMBER MAYFIELD HEWETT is a sought-after event planner and entertaining expert, best known as the founder of the supper club To Be Hosted and the creator of *While Entertaining* on Substack. Amber has helped plan parties for top brands including Bravo TV, Pinterest, and Spotify. Her passion for thoughtfully curating events and generously documenting tips for home hosts earned her a spot on the *Forbes* 30 Under 30 list. Top media outlets, including *The New York Times, Good Morning America,* and *Vogue,* turn to Amber for expert guidance on party planning and hosting. In all that she does, she is on a mission to create more interesting and meaningful social gatherings. When she is not planning parties professionally, she is hosting at home with her husband (and her dog) in the Hudson Valley region of New York. Keep up with Amber on Instagram, Pinterest, TikTok, and YouTube @ambb_mayy.